How to Keep People
From
Pushing Your Buttons

Albert Ellis

How to Keep People From Pushing Your Buttons

Dr. Albert Ellis
and
Dr. Arthur Lange

A Citadel Press Book
Published by Carol Publishing Group

Carol Publishing Group Edition, 1997

A Citadel Press Book
Published by Carol Publishing Group
Citadel Press is a registered trademark of Carol Communications, Inc.

Editorial, sales and distribution, rights and permissions inquiries
should be addressed to Carol Publishing Group, 120 Enterprise Avenue,
Secaucus, N.J. 07094

In Canada: Canadian Manda Group, One Atlantic Avenue, Suite 105,
Toronto, Ontario M6K 3E7

Carol Publishing Group books may be purchased in bulk at special
discounts for sales promotions, fund-raising, or educational purposes.
Special editions can be created to specifications. For details, contact
Special Sales Department, Carol Publishing Group, 120 Enterprise Avenue,
Secaucus, N.J. 07094

Manufactured in the United States of America
10 9 8 7 6 5 4 3 2

Library of Congress Cataloging-in-Publication Data

Ellis, Albert.

How to keep people from pushing your buttons /
by Albert Ellis and Arthur Lange.

p. cm.
"A Citadel Press book."
ISBN 0-8065-1670-4 (pbk.)
1. Interpersonal conflict. 2. Self-control. 3. Interpersonal
relations. 4. Adjustment (Psychology) 5. Rational-emotive
psychotherapy. I. Lange, Arthur J. II. Title.
BF637.I48E45   1994
158'.2—dc20   93-47231
                                        CIP

Contents

A NOTE ON STYLE

In the interest of keeping this book as conversational and accessible as possible, we have included many illustrative first-person anecdotes. Since there are two of us, we have identified ourselves in each instance with the pertinent initials before launching into each personal account. This is why you might see, for example, "I (A.E.) went to the market..." or "I (A.L.) have experienced the following button-pushing incidents...." While we have done our best to present our material in a collaborative manner, we felt that our stories should at least retain such indications of our personal points of view.

Dr. Albert Ellis
Dr. Arthur Lange

Introduction

Today's world can be pretty nutty. And not just at the global level (world events, the economy, social issues), but also in our day-to-day lives. In business, those who still have jobs after all the recent "downsizings" are working more hours. Competition, rapid response to opportunities, change, strategic redirection, risk-taking, doing more with less, and economic constraints are the names of the game.

In our personal lives, both parents in most families work, lots of families break up and recombine as new families, there are zillions of "things" to get done with so little time. (Remember the bubble-bath commercial "Calgon, take me away!"? Fat chance.) The challenges and demands of marriage and parenting can be staggering—and, often, single people have at least as many pressures balancing work, friends, intimate relationships, social activities, and tasks.

It's no wonder that in these times people and things alike can really push our buttons. It can be a person who pushes our buttons: a "know it all" colleague, an overly critical boss, a defensive supervisee, an insensitive spouse, a difficult child, a whiney friend, an indifferent service person, a negative relative. How many times have you heard people say, "I love my job, but my boss drives me nuts!"? Or, "You kids are making me crazy!"? Or, "I just hate it when he always...!"?

Sometimes "they" push our buttons on purpose, and at other times, though it's not even intentional, we still get upset, defensive, hurt, or furious. Sometimes it's a "thing," an event, a task, a decision, a deadline, a change, a crisis, a problem, or an uncertainty. Take for example changing careers, getting divorced or married, buying a house, going on a job interview, speaking in front of a group, traffic, boring meetings, mechanical breakdowns (car, washer, computer), or the babysitter doesn't show up when you have show tickets.

Many of the most popular shows on TV (*Roseanne, Coach, Seinfeld, Frazier, Fresh Prince, Married With Children*) are examples of people pushing each other's buttons constantly. And we can all relate to them. But it doesn't have to be like that! We're *not* suggesting that real life is like *Ozzie and Harriet* or *Leave It to Beaver*! Most of us, however, can do a lot better at *not* letting people and things get to us.

This book gives you specific, realistic ways to keep people and things from pushing your buttons. There's no theoretical mumbo-jumbo and no touchy-feely psychology here—nor is this a shallow "positive-thinking quickie." Rather, it *is* a very specific set of skills for directing *how* you preferably should react when people and things push your buttons. And it works! We have given over 10,000 presentations on these skills, all over the world. They are equally applicable in our work and in all our personal lives. The situations and circumstances may be quite different, but the skills apply *everywhere*.

The goal of this book is to show you how you can live an active, alive, vigorous—even demanding—life and not be a casualty of your own efforts. We will give you a powerful set of skills so that your bosses, colleagues, supervisees, spouses, kids, parents, neighbors, friends, lovers, and other people you deal with day-to-day no longer push your buttons. Rarely do *all* these people get to us *all* the time, but most of us have let *someone* push our buttons *sometime*.

Life is short and precious. We want to help you to succeed at what you are doing *and* enjoy the trip. We will show you *how* to take control of your overreactions to the people and things that push your buttons.

**How to Keep People
From
Pushing Your Buttons**

Chapter 1

How We Let People and Things Push Our Buttons

There are only three things that human beings can do. And you're doing all of them right now. (This eliminates at least some of the things you're probably considering.) You do all three almost all the time, even while you're asleep. First, you are *thinking*. Some of you are thinking about what the three things are. Or maybe you're thinking about something that's coming up tonight, or this weekend; or about what someone just said to you; or what this book is going to be about. But you are almost always thinking something. Sometimes you're not even aware of all your thoughts—but if you stop and pay attention, you can recognize most of them.

Second, you are almost always *feeling* something, and we don't mean hot or cold or tired or pain, we mean emotion. Sometimes it's a mild feeling, like "sort of" irritated, "somewhat" amused, "a little" down, "kind of" happy, or "a bit" guilty. Sometimes it's a very intense feeling, like furious, outraged, elated, thrilled, depressed, bummed out, ecstatic, joyous, freaked out, or "really" guilty. There are enormous numbers of feelings and intensities—but you're almost always feeling something.

Lastly, you *behave* (i.e., *act*) constantly. Even the tiniest gestures and movements, while you are reading this, are behaviors. Did you just blink? Are you breathing? Are you making a face, or shifting in your chair? As long as you are alive, you are behaving.

Now, it's not terribly brilliant of us to point out that human beings think, feel, and act. But it's nevertheless a great place to start, because if we're going to keep people and things from pushing our buttons, we'd better learn how to direct and control the way we *respond* mentally, emotionally, and behaviorally to button-pushers. And that takes both systematic effort, and diligent practice of the skills and techniques we'll soon describe.

This book is not a "quickie" solution to life's day-to-day hassles. The techniques are simple and very powerful, but if you want them to work you have to use them regularly.

The Fatal Foursome

There are four main "screwball" feelings in this world. That is, any time you experience one of these feelings, you will not handle the situation as effectively as you could, and you will probably upset yourself; somebody or something will push your buttons. These feelings are *excessive* anxiety, anger/defensiveness, depression/burn-out, or guilt (we'll tell you what we mean by excessive in just a minute). First, if you get yourself overly *anxious* (or nervous, tense, upset, agitated, intimidated, afraid, freaked out, fearful, scared), you will not handle that person or situation effectively. For example, maybe you get extremely nervous in a job interview, or when talking to an intimidating boss. Maybe you find yourself getting terribly upset about an impending deadline at work, or a major decision in your life, or about your child's behavior lately. If you do, then someone or something *is* pushing your buttons.

Second, if you get overly *angry* (or defensive, irritated, furious, outraged, argumentative, ticked off, frustrated) you will also likely blow it. Maybe you have felt really defensive when your spouse has criticized your work, your cooking, your parenting, or your lovemaking. Maybe you blow up when your teenager defies or disrespects you, or your colleagues at work are incompetent or uncooperative.

Here's an example of a fellow who let his buttons get pushed on a plane going from San Francisco to Los Angeles. This incident occurred just as the laws changed to prohibit smoking on most flights. As I (A.L.) and others boarded the plane, the ticket agent announced that ours would be a totally smoke-free flight. The passenger who was seated next to me did not hear the announcement by the agent and when it was reannounced on the plane, he was really ticked off.

First he tried to get me to agree to his smoking anyway (which I did not do); then he went on for several minutes about how it was *illegal* for the airline to prohibit smoking. He thrashed and wriggled in his seat for several minutes, coughing and sighing. He then pronounced, "this restriction is going to piss off a lot of people"—and proceeded to light up.

The flight attendant immediately came up to him and very politely said, "Sir, this has been designated a nonsmoking flight." He asked, "By whom?" Startled, she replied, "Pardon me?" He repeated—"I *said* by whom?" She said, "The captain." He shot back with, "Well, tell the captain he's a pain in the ass." She asked, "*What* should I tell him?" He then said (as he put his cigarette out angrily), "Tell him he's got no business doing that, and he's a real pain in the ass!" She said, "OK." He then threatened to go into a lavatory (where no smoking is allowed) and have a cigarette. The flight attendant pointed out that this, too, was against the law. He growled and used more foul language—and the flight attendant excused herself.

Interestingly, a little later another passenger nicely asked the same flight attendant about the smoking ban, expressed concern over it, and calmly disagreed with the decision. The flight attendant was understanding yet firm, and the passenger was polite. The flight attendant then offered the passenger a free drink for the inconvenience. What a difference between the way the two smokers handled the situation! The first passenger was awfulizing, shoulding, *and* rationalizing (mostly shoulding). The second passenger was thinking in terms of strong preferences, but did not overreact. Neither person got to smoke—but one made himself miserable, and the other got a free drink. I was also really impressed with how the flight attendant did not let either person get to her. In that job you get lots of practice in not letting people push your buttons!

There are millions of potential button-pushers all around us. Our "mission," if we choose to accept it, is to disconnect our button at will. Then *they* can't get to us unless *we* let them. We don't have to run away and hide from the button-pushers, or play "sticks and stones will break my bones, but names will never hurt me" mind games. We can deal with the button-pushers directly and appropriately, without losing our composure. If you get yourself excessively *depressed* or *burned out* (bummed out, don't give a damn, ignoring, uncaring, down in the dumps), you will not be as effective, and you will likely be miserable. Similarly, if you *persist* in being depressed over the loss of someone you love, or of your job, or for having failed miserably at some effort, then you have in fact let someone or something push your buttons.[1]

Fourth, if you make yourself excessively *guilty* (overly responsible, remorseful, blameful), then others can manipulate you, you will not make as good assessments, and you will make decisions for all the wrong reasons (because you felt so guilty). For example, maybe you let the kids get away with murder because you got a divorce and you feel guilty about having done that to them; or you spend too much of your personal time with someone you don't really like because "you're the only friend they have"—and you feel like a louse if you neglect him or her.

A key concept here derives from the word *excessive*. But what *is* "excessive"? When, say, are your emotions excessive? It's such a subjective concept! Actually, though, we would bet that 85 percent of the time, you can tell exactly when you are overreacting. Sometimes you don't like to admit it, but you can tell. If someone were to tap you on the shoulder when you were having an outburst, and ask nicely, "Aren't you overreacting?" you might snap back "Yeah—what's it to you?" But you *do know*. It might be hard to admit it, but you can figure it out.

---

[1]You may have noticed that we used the terms *depression* and *burnout* together. We did because they often look the same. If you described someone who was burned out, how would you describe that person (bored, listless, flat affect, unproductive, doesn't care about things he or she used to care about)? If we asked you to describe someone who was depressed, you might give a very similar description. They are often very much alike, and we've all felt like this about someone or something.

Naturally, sometimes you have strong feelings, and it's not always clear whether they seem appropriate in their intensity or are an overreaction. But most of the time you can figure it out—you know exactly when you are overreacting.

Therefore, "excessive" here means that *by your own judgment* you overreacted.[2] The real task is what to *do* about it: How to keep as many as possible of these overreactions from happening in the first place, how to get rid of them quickly and prevent them from recurring in the future. Sometimes it takes courage to admit you are overreacting instead of putting the blame on someone or something else. We'll soon show you how to prevent that kind of blame-shifting mental gymnastics, too.

The ABC's of Button-Pushing

Here are the A's. (These are the pushers.) In order to keep people and things from pushing your buttons, you start by figuring out what *really* causes your reactions in the first place. The best way to understand how we let them get to us is to use a model that I (A.E.) developed in 1955, when I started to practice Rational Emotive Behavior Therapy (REBT), the first of today's cognitive behavior therapies. It's called the ABC's. A's represent specific people and things (Activating Events) that we run into on a day-to-day basis that could push our buttons.

There are two kinds of Activating Events. Sometimes, A's are major crises like flood, famine, disease, or locusts. Actually, we tend to rise to the occasion for the biggies; people show amazing ability to handle extremely traumatic situations. Flood and earthquake victims do incredible things to stay alive in the crisis, and then to pull together to rebuild both their lives and their communities. We know these deeds are true because we read about them in (for an exaggerated example) the *National Enquirer:* "Woman lifts tractor-

---

[2]Caution: Don't use other people's opinions of your behavior. ("Oh, you're just overreacting") if *you* don't truly agree. Sometimes they *are* right, but sometimes they are just being manipulative to get you to do what they want you to do. Use your own judgment!

trailer, saves child's life underneath!" It *is* true that we can do all kinds of things during the biggies!

It's the *second* kind of Activating Event (A) that we let get to us. It's the daily hassles, frustrations, worries, problems, decisions, and difficult people that we allow to do the job on us. They chip away at us, one by one. None of them is a big deal by itself, but they sure can add up and take their toll.

For example, the button-pushers (the A's) on and about your job might be the constant interruptions, the frequent deadlines, the difficult bosses, supervisors and colleagues, freeway traffic, office politics, incompetence (usually in others), unnecessary paperwork, changes in policy or procedures, know-it-alls, irresponsibility, laziness, negativity, personality clashes, massive egos, whiners, losing a promotion, getting a promotion, being criticized unfairly, not being appreciated, heavy workload, boring/endless meetings, frequent discrepancies between what you *must* do and what you *think* is right, uncertainty about how well you're doing, being held responsible but with little authority, dealing with a difficult customer, the public, vendors, and/or people from other departments. Whew!

You might make a list of *your* button-pushers on the job. We all have them, and most of them are minor—but the list can get mighty long. Use the appropriate sheets in the following exercises section to get started, then keep adding to your own lists.

In your personal life the button-pushers (the A's) might be dealing with your children, conflicts with your spouse or lover (or both!), the workload at home, equipment breakdowns (cars, appliances, answer machines), money problems, going through a divorce (or the flip side, marriage),[3] moving, redecorating, dealing with the IRS, difficult relatives or neighbors, constant phone salespeople, poor service, selfish/insensitive friends, a serious illness or death in the family, or a birth in the family. Notice that some of these events (A's) are positive and some are negative. They all, good or bad, have the potential to push our buttons. Notice, too, that some situations are the flip side of

---

[3]Once in a workshop when I (A.L.) asked for examples of A's, someone in the audience said, "Divorce." I replied, "And on the flip side?" and she said, "Death!"

each other: divorce/marriage; getting promoted/losing a promotion; a birth in the family/a death in the family. We have the capacity to overreact to almost anything! We don't all overreact to the same things, nor do we all run into the same situations (A's), but we do all have our own individual set of button-pushers (A's).

Sometimes the A's are a whole series of events that go wrong. Here is a real-life version of the movie *Planes, Trains, and Automobiles* (starring Steve Martin and John Candy) that actually happened. Several years ago I (A.L.) was invited to give the opening address to a conference of 400 psychologists from all over the world, in Munich, West Germany. This was a real honor, and I jumped at the chance. I started out on my trip from southern California two days before the conference was to begin. As it turned out, it took me 47 hours to go from Los Angeles to Munich! (Whether or not you've ever made the trip, it's not supposed to take that long.)

I started out, very early in the morning, driving up to Los Angeles International Airport and its West Imperial Terminal, where the charter flights gather. I walked up to the ticket agent, who said "Oh yes, Dr. Lange, that flight has been delayed 29 hours; it hasn't even left Frankfurt yet." (He said this with a tiny little smile at the corners of his mouth.) I was just starting to catch the full impact of his words as my first question came: "Why didn't you call me and let me know? I have to be in Munich!" He said, "Gee, there were a lot of people on that plane—I couldn't call everybody." I started seeing red.

I was getting really fired up now, but what could I do (short of a tantrum or punching the agent)? Nothing *there.* So, I drove all the way home, called my travel agent (a friend), and told him, "I've got to get a flight to Munich *today!*" He said, "Well, I'll see what I can do, but they don't exactly grow on trees. I'll call you right back." A few minutes later he did and reported, "I've got some good news and some bad news. The good news is that I've booked you on a flight to Copenhagen with connecting flights to Hamburg and Munich. The bad news is that your *round-trip* charter fare was $450. This is going to cost you $785 *one way.* Do you want it? By the way, if you do, you have to get back up to LAX [L.A. Airport] fast, because the first flight is taking off in one hour and a half."

The conference coordinators agreed to pay my charter flight ($225 one way), but I didn't have time to get them to approve this much greater price, so I made an "executive" decision and confirmed the reservation.

I rushed up to LAX and got on the plane, which taxied out to the runway and *stopped dead*. The pilot came on the public-address system and said, in that classically professional yet casual "pilot" tone of voice, "Folks, we seem to be experiencing a little technical difficulty, but don't worry—if it's anything serious, we'll put you all up at a real fine hotel right here at the airport. We're going back to the jetway and you will deplane; but hang around the area because we may get this problem fixed real fast." My first thought was, "We're going to fly over the North Pole. Take your time, fix it right, don't rush!" My second thought I won't record here.

About three hours later I heard an announcement: "Flight XYZ to Copenhagen ready to board in 15 minutes." We got back on the plane, it took off, and we eventually landed in Copenhagen with no more problems. But now we were three hours late, so I missed my connecting flights to Hamburg and Munich. Nevertheless, I rushed to the gate for the Hamburg flights—and the ticket agent said, "You are in luck! [I rolled my eyes.] Go down this ramp and hurry because the last flight to Hamburg and Munich is just about to leave!"

I rushed down the jetway and got on the plane, which taxied out to the runway and *stopped dead*! The German pilot got on the speaker and said something in German, and the whole planeload went "Arrrrrghhhhhh!" (I'm a psychologist, so instantly I knew something was wrong). I asked another passenger—one who spoke a little English—what the pilot had said. The man said, "We are to get off the plane out here on the tarmac, point to our luggage, which is being removed from the plane, and get back on the plane."[4] I said, "Huh?" He repeated the same statement. I said, "Maybe we're having a language difficulty." He looked me right in the eye and said, "Look, man—we have to get off the plane, point to our luggage, and get back on the plane!"

[4]At this point you might be thinking this is a joke or a put-on. This is a *true* story—and it gets *worse!*

And that's exactly what we all did. It turned out that a group of urban guerrillas had threatened to blow up *a* plane, but they hadn't said *which* one! The airlines immediately instituted a policy requiring visual recognition of all luggage. Our plane was one of the first scheduled to leave after the threat, and had not done the visual check. They were not allowed to leave without it. Now I had two reactions: (1) "It's taken an hour and a half to go through this procedure, and my connecting flight to Munich has been shot again" and (2) "I wonder when the plane is going to blow up." We all got back on board. The plane took off. It eventually landed in Hamburg. No problem.

As I was running through the Hamburg airport, in the hope of catching a last flight to Munich, I was tired and looking a bit worse for wear (I had much longer hair then, and I guess I was downright sleazy). I looked up and saw a dozen huge WANTED posters of members of the urban guerrilla gang posted all over the airport walls. I suddenly realized that I looked like about *nine* of these guys!

Suddenly, two soldiers with machine guns strapped over their shoulders rushed up to me and yelled "Halt!" I stopped about four feet in the air. Apparently, in my haste, I had entered a "No Admittance" area. Since I looked pretty suspicious and these young men were understandably a little nervous about these would-be bombers, they decided to frisk me. They took me into a small room with an officer, and inspected me *carefully* and *thoroughly*. They were looking for a bomb! I can tell you right now, I wouldn't put a bomb where they looked for anything in the world. No cause, no crusade, *nothing* would get me to put a bomb where they checked!

They quickly let me go, and I finally got to the Munich ticket counter. Miracle of miracles, the agent said there was one more flight to Munich, one which had been delayed but was now ready to leave. I got on the plane! It taxied out on the runway and *stopped dead!* The pilot announced (this time in German *and* English) that the flight had been *canceled;* there was fog in Munich, and the plane couldn't land. It could take off fine, but it couldn't land!

We deplaned, and found the ticket agent standing well behind his counter (this was a hostile crowd). He quickly explained that we had two choices: (1) Wait until the next morning (it was then about 11:00 P.M. on the night before I was to give my talk at 8:00 A.M. in the morning), and hope that the fog would lift; or (2) have the airline transfer my ticket to a train—which allegedly would get me to Munich at 8:05 A.M. Again I made an "executive" decision, trading my ticket for the train ostensibly leaving in a half hour.

After taking a taxi across town to the train station, I entered only to find about 40 stairways, each going down to different tracks. At the top of each stairway a sign listed one or two cities. I got to about Track 22, whose sign read "Muenchen." I said to myself, "That's close enough." Just as I started down the stairs, however, the train started pulling out. I literally threw my luggage onto the last steps of the last car and jumped onto the train. I made it!

I sat down with some Canadians and talked for a little while, but now it was well after midnight, and we all decided to get some sleep. We moved to empty compartments in other cars up ahead (the seats on those trains fold down, so you can actually sleep). About 4:00 A.M. I woke up from a sound sleep and felt several strong thumps from the train. I rolled over, thinking, "Nah, nothing else can go wrong." But then thump, thump, thump—again. And the train seemed to be standing still. So I gathered myself up (I had left my luggage in the other car), went down the corridor, opened the door—and *there was nothing there!* It was pitch dark outside, but I could easily see that the rest of the train was gone. I started to get nervous, because (adding to the mystery) no one else was in the car. Totally confused, I suddenly saw a sign on the side of the car that said "Berlin!"[5] At that point, the train started up, so I made my third "executive" decision: I jumped off the moving train. (Believe me, it's not like the old cowboy movies. You really go flying head-over-heels, especially if you can't see beyond your nose. When I got up, I finally realized what I had done. I had left myself standing out in the darkness somewhere in the middle of Germany, with the only light I could see getting smaller and smaller as it faded into the distance.

---

[5]German trains, I've since learned, often are "split in half," the one section then going in one direction (my luggage was doing fine—straight to Munich) while the other goes in a different direction (as with me, to Berlin).

But the Germans are nothing if not observant: About two minutes later, a locomotive went by right near where I was standing, and the engineer must have seen me—because just a few minutes after that two men came running up the tracks (one wore a conductor's hat and a walkie-talkie, and the other a white hard-hat, and held a big club in his hand). I kept yelling "Munich! Munich!" Finally, the conductor looked at the other man and (apparently with me in mind) repeated "Dummkopf! Dummkopf!" I thought to myself, "Now we're communicating!"

The conductor contacted the Munich train (it had only gone around a bend and up to a small train station). I got on, and that train got into Munich at *exactly* 8:05 A.M. The Germans are nothing if not efficient, too.

Now, the conference was being conducted with the assistance of the University of Maryland, which has a campus on an American military base, right in Munich, called McGraw Kaserne. Remember that, through all this misery, I never had a chance to contact the conference people about all the problems and delays. But McGraw Kaserne happens to be a major telecommunications center for the Army, and the conference coordinators knew *exactly* where I was the *whole* time. They knew I'd missed the charter flight, that I'd been on the other two flights, and that I'd switched to the train. The only thing they *didn't* know was that I'd jumped off the moving train. I even had some time on the last leg of the trip to get cleaned up.

When I got off the train in Munich, three people from the conference were there to greet me. They whisked me away in a cab, getting me to the conference in no time. I then walked out on the stage and gave the keynote address at the Stress Management Symposium! Needless to say, I had lots of fresh examples for the presentation. In fact, I used the techniques delineated in this book dozens of times throughout my dismal trip, thus keeping myself from being totally miserable and freaked out. It was still not a "fun" trip, but I honestly handled it well with the help of the four steps we'll be showing you shortly.

Make a list of *your* personal button-pushers, using the appropriate sheets in the following Exercises section. The pushers might be specific people, or single events, or a series of incidents that build up.

They don't have to be major events. They may even seem silly—but if you overreacted, put that down on the list.

Here (to skip the B's for now) are the C's. In the ABC model, C's represent two things: your *feelings* and your *behaviors* in the specific situation occurring at Point A. For example, let's say that (at Point A) you are trying to get to an important meeting or appointment, and you run into some unexpected traffic on the freeway. It isn't quite bumper-to-bumper, but it's slowing down. If you manage to get really anxious, agitated, and angry (your *feelings* at Point C) as you become increasingly late, how might you then start driving (your *behavior* at Point C)? You might weave in and out of lanes, tailgate, drive faster than you would under these conditions, honk your horn, shout at other drivers, and—with the appropriate gesture—show them their IQ. Some people would whip into the car-pool lane and hold up their jacket on the passenger side, hoping the highway patrol wouldn't catch them. Now, if you were not nearly so agitated, would you normally drive like that? Probably not (although some people drive like that all the time). Do you see what happened here?

The first point in this model is: *Feelings* largely *cause behavior.* The *way* you feel, and how strongly, greatly influence how you will behave in a situation. If you get yourself overly anxious, angry, and upset about getting somewhere, you will likely drive like a nut.

Imagine being chosen by your fellow workers to give a major presentation in front of the highest executives in the company, to help convince them to change a policy or procedure, and you are "just" a supervisor, clerk, secretary, or middle manager. Somebody picked you because they wanted the big mucky-mucks to hear from some of the people in the trenches, and you've never done anything like this before. *If* you manage to get yourself excessively emotional, which feeling would it probably be: choose from overly anxious, angry, depressed, or guilty? The most likely is *overly anxious*, since you are about to speak at the head of the 30-foot-long tableful of executives.[6]

---

[6]By the way, the number one phobia (far above all the typical ones like fear of heights, snakes, open spaces, closed spaces, or airplanes) is speaking in front of a group. Number two is close, and all the others are far below: Number two is *death!* Yes, people are more afraid of speaking in front of a group than they are of *dying!* I believe that's true because you often hear people who are asked to speak say, "I wouldn't get up there. I'd be so embarrassed, I'd die!"

How might you then behave? Well, you might fidget, or stumble over the words, or pause often, or talk very fast, or blank out entirely. You see, again, *feelings* usually *cause behavior.* If you were instead walking down the street, calmly talking with a good friend, would you fidget (or whatever)? No—because you wouldn't be anxious. Now, remember, *not* everyone would be excessively anxious when speaking in front of a group. But if *you* were, that would influence how you would act in such a situation. Once more, *feelings* normally *cause behavior!* And, as we shall see later, *behaviors* also *influence feelings.*

If your teenage son or daughter is (perish the thought) being obnoxious for the 4,000th time this week, not sticking to the rules, and being disrespectful or irresponsible, and you finally have had it, how might you talk and act? You might yell, threaten, use abusive language, be demeaning, have a major blowup, or "smack him (or her) good." If you weren't angry, would you behave that way? Probably not. Our feelings usually lead to our behavior.

We could end this book right now if we simply said, "So, if you want to make sure no one and nothing ever pushes your buttons, just don't ever make yourself excessively anxious, angry, depressed, or guilty." Brilliant! Piece of cake! But a little *too* simple. Actually, understanding the role of these four screwball feelings is important, but the critical question is: OK, if feelings cause behavior, *then what causes these feelings?* What causes us to get excessively anxious, angry, depressed, or guilty in the first place? And here is where most people make an incredible mistake: They believe that A's cause C's. And *that* is *not* true!!

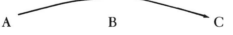

A   B   C

Activating Event: Specific   Your feelings and
situations or people   behaviors

Yet we think in that way, we talk that way, we explain our world that way. If I said to a fellow worker, "Bill, you seem really irritable this morning—what's up?" he might say something like, "Well, I've been stuck on the freeway for the last hour and a half. I was trying to get in here early to prepare for this meeting, and now I have to walk in cold.

It's ruined my whole day already!" He's talking as though A directly caused C, as though A (being stuck on the freeway and having no time to prepare for the meeting) *made* him upset and irritable at Point C. But that is *not* true—even though it *seems* that way.

Let's say you had a fight with your spouse. In reflecting on what happened (especially if you're still angry), you might recall that you said some pretty nasty things, but perhaps quickly explain them by saying, "Well, he started it" or "she made me so mad. . . ." What you would be saying is that his or her behavior (the Activating Event) caused you to act the way you did (at Point C). But that would not be completely accurate: You *also* contributed by what you were thinking about him or her at Point B.

One of my colleagues at work pouted to a fellow worker, "You know that comment you made in the staff meeting? You really ticked me off when you said that. [Pause.] I just wanted you to know that. [Walks away.]" He was saying that the comment made in the staff meeting (Point A) *made* him very angry (at Point C). But (again) A's do *not* directly cause C's—even though we *think* that they do all the time, and it even *seems* like it's really true. We constantly say to our kids, "You're driving me crazy!" But A's by themselves *don't* cause C's.

Well now, if A's *don't* directly cause C's, what *does* cause them? For the most part, B's cause C's. They *interact with* A's to (mainly) cause C's. Killer B's! And they *can* be killer B's if we let them.

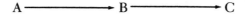

A ────────→ B ────────→ C

Activating Events:	Your beliefs	
Specific situations and	about Activating	Your feelings and
people in situations	Events	behaviors

Here are the B's. So, what *are* B's? What do we do at Point B when we run into a difficult situation or person at Point A *before* we wind up feeling or acting at Point C? There are lots of words to describe what we do at Point B: we react, choose, perceive, decide, analyze, make a judgment, size up the situation, assess it, imagine—all these words and more fall under one rubric, one umbrella term: We THINK! And the way we *think* in response to a specific person or situation will largely determine both how we respond emotionally and behaviorally at Point C, and whether we let the A's push our buttons.

So we see ever more clearly that A's don't cause C's—B's mainly cause C's. Now, some people believe that—especially in sudden situations—they don't think at all; they just react: "As soon as he opened his mouth, I jumped all over him." "I read the memo and 'feathers' instantly hit the fan." "When I heard what they did, I just exploded."

Here's one of the best examples we know to demonstrate that B's cause C's: Imagine that you are in an audience of about 50 people at a lecture that I (A.E.) am giving, and in the middle of the lecture I bring out a large cardboard box, open up the top, and quickly throw the contents of the box out over the whole audience. What I've done is release about 30 of the biggest, fattest rattlesnakes you've ever seen. I'm not talking little bitty garter snakes; I mean muscular Texas rattlers that weave in three directions at once and have giant jaws that open wide, and a forked tongue that shoots out.

Got the picture? What's the *first* thing you would do? Run, yell, scream, jump on your chair, have a heart attack, want to kill me? Those are typical reactions—but technically not accurate. The first thing you would have to do is *see* them. If you were gazing at the clock or the ceiling, or taking notes when I did this, and you didn't see it, you'd look up and think, "Gee, what's everybody yelling about?" Maybe you would hear one of the vipers ("psssssst"), or perhaps one would land in your lap and you'd *feel* it!

Now what am I talking about: seeing, hearing, touching? Your senses! And where does that information go first? To your kneecaps? To your heart? To your feet? ("Feets, don't leave me now!") No, it goes to your *brain,* doesn't it?

Your brain then does two things. First it *labels* the event—calmly, factually, and unemotionally: "Rattlesnakes flying through the air directly at me." Then, your brain makes a *judgment* about that event. That's when it says "Rattlesnakes! Danger! Danger!" and sends that information electrically and chemically through the hypothalamus (a very primitive part of the brain that acts like a traffic cop) to your whole body, signaling it to react to the danger.

Remember that all this happens in micromilliseconds. Those snakes could be halfway through the air and you'd already be three-quarters of the way to the door, all this *thinking* having taken place in between. This is a dramatic example of a sudden event that certainly would push the buttons of most of us—and even here the first thing we did was *think*.[7]

We are going to make a very provocative statement now. It is the second major principle for keeping people from pushing your buttons: *It is not what is actually, verifiably true at Point A that counts, it's what you think about it at Point B that will largely determine how you wind up feeling and acting at Point C.* If you believe it's awful and horrible to screw up, either you will avoid those situations where you *could* screw up (A's), or you will fulfill your own prophecy and *actually* screw up. If you believe you *have to* have someone in your life to make you a truly "whole" person, you will be miserable when you don't, and "they" will be able to push your buttons. If you "can't stand it" when people cut you off on the freeway, you will probably get very upset when they do, and possibly have some nasty exchanges. If you believe that your boss is a terrible person when he or she sets unreasonable deadlines or criticizes you unfairly, you will make yourself miserable on the job. If it "drives you crazy" when your spouse or one of your children is insensitive, irresponsible, or disrespectful, you will let either (or both) of them push your buttons, and you will probably blow it yourself.

What we're saying is that regardless of how valid the situation is, how we *think* about it will really determine how upset we get, and how much we let "it" push our buttons! Now, *that* is both good news and bad news. What if A's (Activating Events) automatically caused C's (our feelings and behaviors)? We would be in deep trouble. Why?

---

[7] I had an interesting reaction from one person in an audience to the question "What would you do if I threw the snakes into the group?" He said in a distinct Texas drawl, "I'd pick 'em up." I said, "C'mon, what are you trying to be, macho man?"—and he explained that as a boy he'd lived on a ranch where they raised rattlers for a roadside tourist attraction. He *thought* about this situation differently. He believed he had a better chance of being safe by picking them up carefully than by running out of the room and stepping on one by mistake. In this case, it was because of his past experience, and what he told himself (at Point B) about it.

Because our reactions would be totally out of our control. However, since the way we *think* at this point about the person or situation really determines how we handle it, we then have the *potential* to control our responses and not let people and things push our buttons. That is the good news.

The bad news is that we also have to take *responsibility* for our feelings and behaviors at Point C. We can't actually say to ourselves: "She upset me" or "He makes me so mad I could wring his neck" or "I'm depressed because I'm going through a divorce" or "Work is getting to me" or "My personal life is ruining me" or "The kids drag me down." Sometimes we even justify our own overreactions by placing the blame on other people, or on things that are happening to us ("Anybody would have reacted that way"). It's just not true. A's by themselves *do not* cause C's.

This business of taking responsibility for our feelings and behaviors is very important. First, we do *not* mean that you should blame or attack yourself for your poor behavior. The trouble is that we often use the terms *responsibility, blame,* and *fault* as though they were interchangeable—but they actually have very different meanings. Responsibility means that *you* are accountable for your feelings and actions, because *you* have the capacity to direct and control them. Blaming yourself means that you put yourself, your entire person, down for having acted badly. Taking responsibility is healthy; blaming yourself is destructive.

Additionally, when we say that what you *think* is true determines how you feel and act at Point C, we are *not* saying that if you think you can fly, and so you jump off a ten-story building, you will glide gently to the pavement. No, you will splat just like everyone else. But if you take even this extreme example to its logical absurdity, if you *really* think you can fly, you might just go up there and foolishly try.

Moreover, we are *not* talking here about the value of positive thinking—which is indeed laudable nevertheless because it tends to motivate people to try things that they might not typically attempt.[8]

---

[8]Positive thinking surely beats negative thinking. But sometimes it can be a con or a distortion of reality. Sometimes the objective affirmations we are encouraged to tell ourselves are just a bunch of subjective baloney. There is a third option: realistic thinking.

We are simply saying that what you *think* in a specific situation will determine both *how* and *how strongly* you respond to that situation (and any people in it).

A good example of how B's largely cause C's can be taken from the Harlem Globetrotters basketball team. During their great performances, two Trotter players invariably get into a mock argument over one's hogging of the ball. The animated exchange escalates to where one player throws a glass of water in the other's face, whereupon the violated player runs over to the bench, picks up the *team bucket* (in which who knows what unpleasant contents might be swirling) and chases his adversary toward the audience. At the last moment the player being chased ducks, and the one with the bucket heaves the contents into the audience. The reactions of the kids in the crowd beautifully prove that B's cause C's.

There are two totally different responses: The kids who have seen the skit before, and so know that confetti is in the bucket, stick their chests and jaws out and yell, "Go ahead!" "Heave-ho!"—while the kids who have not witnessed it duck behind the others and cover their heads. The situation (A) is exactly the same, yet the feelings and behaviors at Point C are totally different. What *was* different for the two groups was their *thinking*, in this case their expectations. A's don't cause C's: B's largely cause C's.[9]

Finally, we are *not* suggesting that people should never feel strongly about anything. What we are saying is that we often overreact as a matter of course to situations and/or people that (to us, at least) are frustrating—but we make things much worse by the *way* we think about them. At that point, *we* are *part* of the problem. Strong feelings are fine; it's the overreactions that mess us up.

George Carlin, the comedian, gave a great example on T.V. when he was making fun of the "affirmations movement" people who always ask: "Is the glass half empty or is it half full?" He said, "Frankly, I think the glass is too *big!*" He is not positive *or* negative, he's a realist!

[9] I don't know if the incident really ever occurred, but several people have reported that *one time* the Globetrotters put *real* water in the bucket—and boy, were those youngsters with their chests sticking out surprised!

EXERCISES

Exercise 1A: Becoming Aware of Your Inappropriate Feelings and Behaviors

When you use the concepts in this book to help yourself stop pushing your buttons, you have at your disposal a number of cognitive, emotive, and behavioral exercises. You can use several of them to discover what your appropriate and inappropriate feelings are, which rational (and irrational) beliefs you are accepting and creating to produce these feelings (which we shall explain in the following chapters), and how to dispute or challenge your irrational ideas and thereby change your emotional overreactions (which we shall *also* explain a little later on). As here, at the end of each chapter of this book (except the last) we provide a few exercises for you to do in order to understand and identify your thoughts, feelings, and behaviors. You can also use these exercises to change them when you have let people and things push your buttons.

The first exercise you can do is watch yourself for the next week to see when, where, and how you experience any of the five undesired feelings and behaviors we described in this chapter: (1) excessive anxiety or worry; (2) excessive anger or defensiveness; (3) excessive depression or burnout; (4) excessive guilt; and (5) any overreactive, self-defeating behavior. Immediately following is a sample worksheet (we call it a practice sheet) you can use to help you to do this.

Sample Practice Sheet for Exercise 1A: Becoming Aware of Your Inappropriate Feelings and Behaviors

Day	Inappropriate Feelings or Behaviors (C's)	Events (A's) That Preceded These Feelings or Behaviors
6/3	Excessive anger; screaming and yelling at son.	Son refused to get up and get ready for school, and I was running late.

6/3	Panic; defensiveness; later, very guilty with boss.	With an irritated, exasperated tone, boss demanded to know when a long and tedious report was going to be finished.
6/3	Excessive anger; hostility toward colleagues.	People from other departments have not sent the information needed for the report.
6/4	Depression.	Received low performance evaluation and low merit-pay increase.
6/6	Procrastination—finding other smaller and less important tasks to do.	Starting to work on the big report.
6/7	Overate (or drank) too much at lunch.	Still not getting much of the report done by lunchtime.
6/7	Uptight; upset stomach; more procrastination.	Overate at lunch, and having to face the miserable report again.
6/7	Having a nasty fight with spouse.	The report is still nowhere near completion, and spouse criticizes your mood lately.

Your Practice Sheet for Exercise 1A: Becoming Aware of Your Inappropriate Feelings and Behaviors

Day	Inappropriate Feelings or Behaviors (C's)	Events (A's) That Preceded These Feelings or Behaviors
—	_____	_____
—	_____	_____
—	_____	_____
—	_____	_____
—	_____	_____
—	_____	_____
—	_____	_____
—	_____	_____

Exercise 1B: Distinguishing Between Your Inappropriate and Appropriate Feelings and Behaviors

You can learn to distinguish between your appropriate (self-helping) and inappropriate (dysfunctional) feelings and behaviors by asking yourself questions like: "Will it help my relationships with others?" "Will it affect my health?" "Will it help me fail or succeed at my goals?" "Will it help or hinder others who are important to me?" "Will this feeling help me get most of what I want, and less of what I don't want?" "Will it get me into any trouble, now or later?"

Make a list of your current inappropriate feelings and behaviors, and one of what you think would be appropriate ones to change them into.

Sample Practice Sheet for Exercise 1B: Distinguishing Between Inappropriate and Appropriate Feelings and Behaviors

Day	Inappropriate Feelings or Behaviors (C's)	Appropriate Substitute Feelings or Behaviors
6/3	Excessive anger; screaming and yelling at son.	Frustration. Firmly and *calmly* tell him what I want him to do, and the consequences if he doesn't. Then carry them out if he still refuses. No yelling or hostility.
6/3	Panic; defensiveness; later, guilty with boss.	Concern over his urgency, and commitment to myself to get the job done.
6/3	Excessive anger; hostility toward colleagues.	Legitimate frustration and request for the needed information quickly; get commitment from them and "buy-in."
6/4	Depression.	Serious concern and disappointment. Find out what the basis is and correct it, or *discuss* it nondefensively with the boss if I disagree.

6/6	Procrastination—finding other smaller and less important tasks to do.	Break the larger report into specific segments, and start working on what I *can* do now.
6/7	Overate (or drank too much) at lunch.	Take a positive break by having a light lunch with a friend and talking about something *pleasant*.
6/7	Uptight; upset stomach; more procrastination.	Diligently chip away at each step of the project, completing what I can—but staying focused.
6/7	Having a nasty fight with spouse.	Talking briefly about the unpleasantness of this task at work; getting some support; enjoying the rest of the evening together.

Your Practice Sheet for Exercise 1B: Distinguishing Between Your Inappropriate and Appropriate Feelings and Behaviors

Day	Inappropriate Feelings or Behaviors	Desired Appropriate Substitutes
____	_____	_____
____	_____	_____
____	_____	_____
____	_____	_____
____	_____	_____
____	_____	_____
____	_____	_____
____	_____	_____

Exercise 1C: Confronting Difficult People and Situations That I Am Likely to Let Push My Buttons

If you find yourself frequently *avoiding* Activating Events (A's) that you would let push your buttons, you will probably not overreact as often *but* you will be doing nothing to change and to get control of the underlying thinking that is at the heart of your upsetness. You aren't handling it any better—you just pushed it under the rug. That type of short-term solution can only work for so long. Then you either explode (from gunnysacking) or you have restricted yourself so much that you're not taking any risks, not asserting yourself, and not improving anything (least of all yourself). If you avoid an obnoxious coworker, you will rarely upset and incense yourself over that person, but you will not have changed your belief ("What a jerk! He *should* not be so obnoxious, and I can't stand it when he is!") to a realistic preference ("I'd like him not to be so obnoxious, but he is. That's frustrating, but I *can* stand it.").

A better plan often is to test yourself out when you might well let certain people and things push your buttons by deliberately approaching or staying with them instead of avoiding them. Then you can desensitize yourself to annoying people and situations *in vivo* (live!), and behaviorally *practice* not upsetting yourself about them. To do this, look for frustrating conditions at work, at home, and socially—and deliberately confront some (not all) of them when this is feasible and is not likely to result in real harm but *is* likely to provide the opportunity for you to work on your own *reactions* (consequences) to adversities (Activating Events) in your life. For example, to help you practice dealing with them appropriately rather than avoid them, make a list of some difficult people and situations you can confront.

Sample Practice Sheet for Exercise 1C: Difficult People and Situations
I Will Soon Try to Confront

1. Being firm yet calm with my son, instead of just ignoring his behavior and repetitiously pleading with him to hurry up.
2. Talking with the boss nondefensively about some of the stumbling-blocks to getting the report completed, and what is a realistic deadline, versus silently taking the heat and fuming inside.
3. Confronting my colleagues with both my need for information and their slow response to that need, while explaining the urgency and importance of getting a commitment from them to deliver, versus complaining about them to others.
4. Working systematically on the report, versus procrastinating.
5. Having a pleasant evening with my spouse, versus fighting about his/her mood and sulking in neutral corners.
6. Bringing up and discussing calmly a sensitive issue with my spouse that might typically lead to defensiveness.
7. Disagreeing with an especially intimidating person.

Your Practice Sheet for Exercise 1C: Difficult People and Situations I
Will Soon Try to Confront

Chapter 2

Nutty Beliefs We Use to Let Others Push Our Buttons

Let's get back to our B's! There are four main ways that you can *think* in any situation at Point B. Again, that's good news and bad news. The good news is that there are *only* four ways, and all are easy to recognize and remember. The bad news is that three of the four ways that you *could* think stink. By this we mean that if you think in any of those three ways, you *will* likely overreact, *will not* handle the situation as effectively as you could, and *will* allow someone or something to push your buttons. The odds are against us—we're human, and so can't perform like a machine, and don't always think in the most functional manner. The goal, though, is to get better at choosing *how* we think, feel, and act with certain people and in specific situations that previously have pushed our buttons. To do that requires two steps: first understanding how you upset yourself, and then how to change your overreactions.

The first of the three main screwball types of thinking at Point B is called *catastrophic* thinking. That's a ten-dollar word which simply means that we catastrophize about all kinds of things. We make them into a bigger deal than they are. Many catastrophic thoughts begin with the phrase "What if...." For example, let's say that you are waiting in the outer office, about to go into an important job interview. What are some of the "what ifs" you might think to yourself that by the time you get in there could make you a nervous wreck? "What if they ask me a question I can't answer? What if I'm not qualified? What if I'm overqualified? What if they don't like me? What if I don't say what they want to hear? What if I don't get the job? What if I *do* get the job?" And so on. These questions strongly imply that if *any* of these things happen it would *not* just be something of concern but a real disaster—panic time. By the time you got into the interview, with this type of thinking you would already be a basket case.

Teenagers are great at catastrophic thinking: "What if my heart's desire doesn't like me? What if I fail the test? What if I don't make the team? What if I'm not popular? What if my friends find out about...? What if they think I'm a geek? What if I look ugly or funny?" And they learn much of it from us—only *we* are more sophisticated (sneaky) about showing it; we're not as transparent.

Adults also catastrophize in their personal and love lives. Let's say you are having some serious trouble with your spouse or lover (or both). You might start thinking: "What if he doesn't love me anymore? What if I'm not attractive to her? What if he is seeing someone else? What if I wind up alone and lonely the rest of my life? What if I stay in this relationship and I'm miserable? What if he doesn't change like he said he would? What if she is bored with me? What if I'm really too old/young for him/her? What if it doesn't get any better? What if we always keep fighting? What if work will always come before *us?*" These are just some of the multitudinous "what ifs" that we can think to ourselves in specific situations, and they all can be extremely upsetting. But before you learn how to change and control catastrophic thinking, it's helpful to understand both what it *is* and what it is *not*.

Not every "what if" thought is necessarily catastrophic. For example, when waiting for a job interview you might think, "What if they ask me what I think my strengths are?" You might sensibly answer by listing these strengths in your head. Or the teenager might think, "What if I don't make the team?" and might answer by deciding "I'll try my very best and if I don't make it, either I'll practice harder and try out again next time, or I'll try out for another team or activity." Or, when meeting an attractive person you would like to date, you may think, "What if we have nothing in common?" And you may answer by concluding either that your differences might be quite interesting, or that it might actually not work out, but you could handle that.

All these first thoughts have started with "What if," but none has been a catastrophic thought. What makes a "what if" thought a catastrophic one is not the question, but rather the *answer:* "What if I don't get the job? *That would be awful!*" "What if I don't make the team? *I couldn't stand it!*" "What if he's not interested in me? *I'd be so embarrassed, I'd die!*" It's the *answers* to the "what ifs" that make them catastrophic. That's why we call this type of thinking *"awfuliz-ing."* When your answer to the "what if" is *"That would be awful!"* (or any such response), you probably are awfulizing. (We prefer to use the word "awfulizing" rather than "catastrophizing" because it more clearly conjures up the image of this type of overreaction.)

"What if-ing" is not the only form of awfulizing. Some people get themselves fired up by often thinking phrases like, "It drives me crazy when...," "I can't *stand* it when...," "It really kills me when...," and "I just hate it when...." Whenever you think these kinds of thoughts, you will likely make yourself susceptible to a person or situation that can really push your buttons.

Awfulizing is a truly great way to upset yourself and make yourself miserable. How many times have you awfulized about something that, by the time it actually happened, wasn't nearly as bad as all the awfulizing you did? We've all done that sometimes. I (A.L.) even had one person say to me indignantly, "Well, so what—it all worked out in the end, didn't it?" I said, "Sure, 'it' [the A] worked out fine, but how did *you* like the trip?"

Yes—how did *you* like making yourself miserable during the time you were awfulizing about that deadline, or that decision, or that relationship? It seems so *natural* to awfulize that we almost assume that it's the *only* way we can react in some circumstances. But that is just not true! It's natural (and almost automatic) to awfulize in some situations, and some of us do it more often than others. But we can all learn how to *stop* indulging ourselves in such emotional overreactions.[10]

Besides being miserably upset, why else would it be better not to awfulize? If you are awfulizing about a person or situation, are you thinking clearly and logically? No! Are you likely to make good decisions? No! If you don't overreact, obviously, you will likely handle the person or situation better. More importantly, you will be taking better care of yourself, and you will not let other people and things push your buttons. *How* to do that is the key.

We are *not* saying that you are supposed to be emotionless, totally unfeeling or robots. That's the ridiculous opposite extreme of over-reacting. There's plenty of room in between for lots of reasonable and appropriate feelings and reactions without letting people and things overly upset you. Can you see how awfulizing sets you up to let people and things push your buttons? We will show you how to attack and change that nutty thinking—but first we'd better know all the "enemies."

The second type of screwball thinking is called *absolutist* thinking, another ten-dollar term. Absolutist thoughts come out in the following forms: "I *must*...," "I *should*...," "I've *got* to...," "I *need* to...," "I *have* to...," "I *ought* to...," and the like. Some of us walk around all day long getting on our own cases: "I've *got* to do this. I've *got* to do that. I *should* have said this to that person. I *need* to be more that. I *ought* to be more organized. I *should* be more attractive, intelligent, witty, popular, and personable. I *ought* to be more assertive. I *need* to be less aggressive. I've *got* to speak up more. I really *need* to keep my mouth shut." And so on.

Some of us "should on ourselves" all day long! That's right! We all *should* on ourselves, constantly getting on our own cases. We don't

[10]In fact, some things in life can *really* be extremely bad or catastrophic—like a slow, painful death; a tragic event like an earthquake; or a major social injustice. Still, awfulizing about them rarely produces a substantive contribution or change. *Doing* something about them, when that's feasible, *can* be productive. But if you're running around like a chicken with your head cut off, getting yourself *excessively* anxious and angry, you will likely become part of the *problem.*

all should on ourselves to the same extent, nor for the same reasons, but we all do it in various ways nevertheless. We can be extremely self-critical, and *that's* what shoulding is. We do it over our looks: "I should have a shorter..., bigger..., firmer..., longer...,"—use your imagination!

We hold ourselves up to people like Cindy Crawford, Niki Taylor, Kim Basinger, Whitney Houston, Matt Dillon, Tom Cruise, Denzel Washington or Patrick Swayze. No question that they are among "the beautiful people." But do we have to should on ourselves if we don't compare adequately? No! Yet we do so, often—and not just on looks. We should on ourselves if we screw up, if we get rejected, if we don't stand up to someone, if things don't go the way we want them to.

We tell ourselves: "I *should* be more intelligent, mature, creative, ambitious, stable, uninhibited, self-directed, logical, intuitive, articulate, knowledgeable, confident, decisive, clever, and or humorous." We *should* either lighten up or be more serious. We *should* grow up fast, mature gracefully or never age at all. We *should* know our place or do our thing. Whatever "it" is, we definitely *should* do it.

Do you know what happens when you are up to your eyeballs in shoulds? Well, first of all, you're *full of should!* But sometimes it runneth over, and then *you* should on somebody *else* that day: "*You* know what you need...," "*You* should be more...," "What *you've* got to do is...," "*You* simply must...." Some of us are simply great at shoulding on other people. A boss gets "shoulded on" by *his* boss, so he shoulds on someone he supervises—and so on, down the line. It's the "trickle-down" theory of shoulding, until someone at the bottom goes home and kicks the cat or takes it out on a helpless family member.

Worse yet is the shoulding we do on ourselves, mentally. It's the kind that enables others to push our buttons. But *how* and *where* did we learn to should on ourselves? Actually, we are constantly bombarded, and thus indoctrinated, with shoulds. Typically, this all starts at home, with our parents. "You should play nicer with your brother." "You should want to be a doctor [or a lawyer or an Indian chief]." "You should be unselfish." "You should turn out the way I think you should." "You should be a brain in school, and a five-letter athlete, and a solo performer in the band at halftime. And don't forget, you *should* be popular."

Then our teachers and our religious representatives take their turns: "You should get good grades, and be disciplined and well-mannered and moral, and decent and kind." Actually, these often are fine goals; it's the *way* they are conveyed (shoulding) that's a problem.

But do you know one of the most insidious sources of shoulding? Television! And we don't mean only the programs, we mean the commercials, too. Sometimes we acquire their subtle shoulds subliminally: "You should have this product, because if you don't, terrible things will happen to you. You will be a failure, or someone will reject you, or *worse*."

One TV commercial goes something like this: There's a good-looking guy who gets off a merchant-marine ship. He's walking down the gangplank wearing his pea jacket, his pea hat, his pea dufflebag, his pea pants. He gets on the dock and two gorgeous women run up, throw their arms around him, and practically molest him—right on TV. He looks up at the boat, and there's *another* good-looking fellow (there *always* are good-looking people in these commercials) standing there, for some reason you'd never guess looking kind of lonely, kind of morose. Instantly, the guy on the dock knows what's wrong. He reaches into his dufflebag and tosses up the famous after-shave. The guy on the ship slaps it on, walks down the gangplank—and two other gorgeous women run up, and throw their arms around *him*. In the next scene this same guy's walking down the road, flanked by his two new friends, and he sees a *third* fellow—sitting at an outdoor restaurant—looking kind of lonely, kind of morose. As the seaman walks by, he slips the sad sack the after-shave. Instantly, yet *another* gorgeous woman sits down at his table! He didn't even put the stuff on! All you have to do is have it near you!

Now, you know that's all just a bunch of baloney. We know a guy who took a *bath* in this stuff, and it didn't do a darn thing for him. But the clear message of the commercial is: If you want to be desired by women, you *should* use (need, must have, ought to get) this after-shave.

We also love the toothpaste commercial wherein the teenage

couple is saying goodnight at her doorstep. But he did not brush with the right toothpaste! He leans toward her to kiss her, and a giant green cloud comes out of his mouth and asphyxiates her—she keels over backward, out cold. He killed his girlfriend with his breath! Then the announcer says something like, "You *should* have [X] toothpaste, or you will really blow it in these crucial moments."

Then there is the commercial with the handsome fellow walking down the aisle of a bus and seeing a lovely woman seated next to an empty seat. He thinks (via voice-over), "There she is again this morning. Maybe I'll sit down next to her!" She looks up with a big smile and obvious anticipation—but at the last second, *she inadvertently scratches her head!* And this guy thinks a thought that nobody else in the history of the human race has ever thought. He thinks, "Well, she *is* attractive, but she just *scratched her head!*" And he keeps walking!

This guy ought to be put away! People don't really think that way! The announcer, though, *believes* in the clod. He comes on and says something like: "You may not *have* dandruff, but scratching your head may be the first sign of having dandruff. You *should* get this anti-dandruff shampoo, because you wouldn't want this to happen to you, would you?" Now, tell us—do *you* scratch your head *at least* once a day? Is your head itchy right now just *thinking* about this?

They don't sell only cosmetic and other personal-appeal products this way. They sell *anything* by convincing us we *should* have the product. There's a coffee commercial in which one couple goes to another couple's house for dinner, and the hostess says, "Bob, would you like a second cup of coffee?" I have no idea why, but Bob's wife answers for him. The whole commercial would end right there if Bob would only say to his wife, "Hey, she asked *me.*" But his wife says, almost smugly, "Oh, Bob *never* takes a second cup of *my* coffee." Bob takes a quick look at his wife and smilingly says to the lovely hostess. "Sure, I'd love some." Bob's wife is now going into cardiac arrest. Her voice-over thoughts are, "Bob *never* takes a second cup of *my* coffee!"

The next scene is of Bob and his wife the next morning, in their breakfast nook, having a second cup of coffee—and even a third cup! He's already had an excess dose of caffeine and missed his first two appointments, but everything is wonderful. The whole message (which is also quite sexist) is: "If you want to be a thoroughly adequate and providing spouse, you *should* get this coffee—because if you don't, somebody else will [and you know where *that* could lead]!" We know it's a ridiculous suggestion, yet they sell this product by the tank-car load.

What really concerns us, though, is the subtle way we are taught to *should on ourselves* and worry about what *others* think. We are constantly encouraged to question how adequate we are. To a point, there's nothing wrong with evaluating what we do. But so many people overdo it and wind up shoulding on themselves *and others* about too many things. The worst thing about awfulizing and shoulding is that we then make ourselves incredibly susceptible to other people's pushing our buttons—which is when we give them tremendous power.

I (A.L.) live in southern California, in an area where shoulding *on* people is an art form. So many people there run around worrying about how they stack up on the status pecking order! The first thing out of their mouths when you meet them is name-dropping some-thing—*anything:* "I was driving in my new BMW [or Mercedes or Porsche] the other day, and there was a lot of traffic." You stand there with a blank stare, wondering what the point is, until you realize it was to remind you of his or her new Beamer. You think, "Frankly, Scarlett. . . . " But they work the impressive facts in somehow, anyway.

Other people have to check you out when they first meet you: "Oh, hello—where do *you* live?" "Oh, but what *section?*" "Oh, well—do you live in the tract homes or the custom Presidentials, where *we* are?" "Oh. But do you have a *view?*" Eventually, after you finally answer a question that reveals you are not as good as the questioner, the "Oh" sounds much less interested, and infinitely more disapprov-ing. I work regularly on not letting them push my buttons in these ways.

Let's take New York, where I (A.E.) live and where shoulding is also a fine art. At a Long Island party, I met a fellow who whispered to me that George (his neighbor) was one of the "original" owners in their section of homes. At first I thought he was saying that being an "original" made George "good" (like he was a Founding Father or was on the Mayflower), but his tone of voice seemed disapproving. So I naively asked him what he meant. With a look of mild surprise (as though I should have clearly understood) he explained, "Well, George paid under a fourth of what the rest of us paid to live in this neighborhood at today's values. He's really not in the same financial ballpark." Can you believe it? This guy was bragging about having paid four times more than George for the same type of house, and his was 15 years older when he bought it! I *should* be impressed that he could afford it, and George *should* feel like he's less of a person! That's classic shoulding!

These have been a few "homely" examples of the nastiness of shoulding *on each other.* Shoulding *on ourselves* is the worst kind of overreaction because we make ourselves miserable *and* we make ourselves susceptible to button-pushers.

The third type of screwball thinking is the exact opposite extreme: *rationalization.* Rationalizations are *underreactions.* They are poor attempts to deny or play down what is happening. They come out in the form of such thoughts as "Who cares?" "Big deal!" "Doesn't bother me." and "So?" They are attempts to deny that we have any reaction at all. Actually, they are cons—and with their use we are trying to con *ourselves!*

When rationalizing, we hold our feelings in and try to deny them, even to ourselves. Let's say you are going through an unwanted divorce. If you were trying to downplay the situation, you might tell yourself a series of rationalizations, like those listed above. In fact, you may have *some* legitimate feelings (although it's *not* awful, terrible, and horrible, and you *can* stand it), but your rationalizations often go to the opposite extreme and don't allow for *any* reaction. Rationalizations may "work" for a very short time, but they leave you vulnerable to the thing that is pushing your buttons—because you never really deal with it.

Parents sometimes reach the point with a difficult child (let's say a son) where they think, "I've had it. He can go to hell in a hand-basket for all I care. I give up—if he wants to ruin his life, let him go ahead. Doesn't bother me. I quit." Usually this happens just after they've been awfulizing and shoulding a whole lot. After rationalizing for a day or so, they usually go back to awfulizing and shoulding again. They go from one extreme to the other.

Other people try to comfort themselves, when (say) they haven't gotten a promotion, by thinking "Who cares? Big deal. Ha, that's their loss. Doesn't bother me that those jerks can't recognize talent. I probably wouldn't like the job, anyway." We think they protest too much!

Some rationalization is pure sour grapes, whether it be over losing a promotion, not getting hired, being rejected romantically, not having friends, not getting elected (to—for example—public office, lodge Grand Poohbah, charity ball chairperson, or pep-squad captain), or not reaching a desired financial or popularity level. We also rationalize our fears with excuses: "Oh, it's just not the right moment to ask for the raise." Or, "There are too many people around just to go up to that person and introduce myself."

We can rationalize incredibly to justify unethical or inappropriate behavior, and thereby con ourselves into accepting our actions: "Everybody cheats in this class—it's so easy to get away with it—and besides, the teacher is a real creep. It's no big deal." Psychologists call this type of rationalization *cognitive dissonance*, which means that we will go to some surprising lengths to "make sense out of" or to justify our questionable behavior.

When we rationalize, we are feebly trying to cope with problems. Even in really serious situations we can rationalize. For example, in a study of women who had surgery for breast cancer, the researchers asked a particularly interesting question: "How much time passed between the day you were aware of unusual lumps in your breast and when you finally went to a physician and had them diagnosed?" The *average* for the entire study was six months! Some people waited *years!* When asked why they waited, they hadn't awfulized—they instead gave typical *rationalizations:* "I didn't want to make a big deal out of it." "I figured if I ignored it, it would go away." "I didn't want to be a hypochondriac." "I didn't want to know, anyway!" Waiting six months can be the difference between the removal of a tumor and a radical mastectomy, or even death. Yet we can easily rationalize dealing with it properly.

To cite a somewhat similar example: men who survived their first heart attack were asked a series of sociological questions. One of the answers bowled the researchers over. They asked, "When you realized you were having a heart attack, what did you do?" They were expecting answers like "I called 911" (or "...my wife," "...my minister," "...my broker." *Over a third* of the respondents said they started to do some form of vigorous physical exercise (pushups, jumping jacks, walking up and down the stairs)! Does that make sense? No! But maybe it *does* if you ask yourself whether their behavior was a result of their rationalizing—"I'm *not* having a heart attack. Hell, no! It's just a little gas. No problem; I'll just shake it off." We can be so wary of heart attacks that we deny one if it hits us right in the rib cage.

If we can con ourselves over such serious things, we can surely rationalize away our lesser day-to-day problems. When some*one*—or some*thing*—pushes our buttons, we just don't want to deal with that at all. Rationalizations often are coverups for things that *really* push our buttons. Alas, coverups just don't work. Avoidance and denial simply are not long-term solutions. The shunned problems are still there—and, sure enough, will surface again!

We have now identified the real enemy: the three types of thinking that can keep us from handling button-pushers effectively (awfulizing, shoulding, and rationalizing). Now we can figure out how to get rid of these hindrances and what we can substitute in their place.

EXERCISES

Exercise 2A: Discovering Irrational Beliefs Leading to Your Inappropriate Feelings and Behaviors

Almost every time you let someone or some situation push your buttons, you are strongly having—at Point B in the ABC's—either conscious or unconscious irrational beliefs. You can have scores of these irrational beliefs at one time, and thousands during your lifetime. But they all can be put under four major headings: (1) shoulding, musting, or demanding; (2) awfulizing or catastrophizing; (3) blaming people rather than their acts; and (4) rationalizing or excusing. Whenever you feel excessively upset, or you're acting dysfunctionally, you will almost always be able to find one or more of these irrational beliefs and then—as we will show later—be able to change and dispute them.

To look for your irrational beliefs, you ask yourself questions like: "When I let my buttons be pushed, what shoulds and musts am I thinking? Am I insisting that *I* must do well, that others *have to* treat me better, that *conditions* have *got to* be the way I want? Am I irrational in believing that it's *awful, terrible,* or *horrible,* or that I *can't stand it* when things go wrong? Am I rationalizing, making up excuses, and (therefore) doing nothing to change things when they are obnoxious? Am I 'what if-ing' myself, and dreaming up horrors that will probably never occur—or that I can really handle if they do happen?"

Make a list of your major excessive feelings and behavioral overreactions. Then ask yourself a question from among those in the previous paragraph. Finally, write down some of your major irrational beliefs by means of which you are largely creating your own button-pushing.

Sample Practice Sheet for Exercise 2A: Discovering Irrational Beliefs
Leading to Your Inappropriate Feelings and Behaviors

Inappropriate Feelings and Behaviors	Irrational Beliefs Leading to These Inappropriate Feelings and Behaviors
Furious with my son in the morning.	He *shouldn't* be such a problem in the morning! I can't stand it! I swear he does it on purpose just to bug me, the little creep! What a mess!
Panic; guilt with demanding boss.	I *should* have finished the report days ago! What's the matter with me? Now I'm really in trouble. This is *awful*, I've really blown it now. Boy, am I stupid!
Upset and depressed over poor performance evaluation.	Now look what's happened! But it's not my fault! The others wouldn't help me, and my boss doesn't understand. It's not fair! I *should* just quit! They're all a bunch of jerks, anyway.
Procrastination on report.	I hate this stupid report. I shouldn't be doing it. Besides, nobody else is doing their share. I'm just too busy with other things to get into it.
Fighting with spouse.	He says I'm moody lately. Huh! What a jerk! He'd be moody too if he had to put up with all the garbage I have to deal with all day, and then come home to more!

Your Practice Sheet for Exercise 2A: Discovering Irrational Beliefs Leading to Your Inappropriate Feelings and Behaviors

Inappropriate Feelings and Behaviors	Irrational Beliefs Leading to These Inappropriate Feelings and Behaviors
_____	_____
_____	_____
_____	_____
_____	_____
_____	_____
_____	_____
_____	_____
_____	_____
_____	_____

Exercise 2B: Invalidating Your Rationalizations and Excuses

Sometimes, instead of admitting the irrational beliefs that led to our emotional and behavioral overreactions, we try to rationalize them away with excuses, cons, denials, and cop-outs. There is usually a grain of truth (which is what is minimally needed to make them plausible) to rationalizations. In fact, however, they are coverups either to justify our actions or to blame someone else. Look for these rationalizations and excuses, and challenge and dispute them (as we shall show you how to a little later).

When you suspect that you may be rationalizing, ask yourself questions like: "Is my explanation for failing, or getting upset, or avoiding this situation a true reason? Am I taking responsibility appropriately, or am I placing blame on someone or something else to avoid failure, rejection, or blame? If I *do* take responsibility for my inappropriate feelings or behaviors, does that make me a bad person because I overreacted? Can I admit to my own feelings and behaviors, and the results they produced?"

You do not have to second-guess yourself constantly, or take responsibility for others, in order to check out the possibility that you are rationalizing. Look for some of your possible rationalizations and excuses, and forcefully question their validity.

Sample Practice Sheet for Exercise 2B: Invalidating Your Rationalizations and Excuses

Possible Rationalization	Challenge to the Rationalization
Maybe my son is just going through a phase, and I should just ignore that he's so uncooperative in the morning.	Am I avoiding dealing with him by vaguely justifying his behavior? Am I anxious that I can't handle it if I do confront him?
This report isn't really that important. Nobody reads them anyway.	Am I trying to justify my procrastination and ignore the fact that the boss *does* care?
My poor performance evaluation is only because I don't play office politics like the others. It has nothing to do with how good a job I'm doing. Everybody couldn't get an excellent rating; I'm just the sacrificial lamb.	Am I avoiding taking responsibility for the poor evaluations? Am I afraid to consider the possibility that I did *not* do as good a job as I could, or as the boss expected?
My husband had it coming to him. He's not supportive; he always takes their side and criticizes me.	Am I justifying starting a fight with him? Am I avoiding the validity of his criticism? Does his behavior justify my overreaction?

Your Practice Sheet for Exercise 2B: Invalidating Your Rationalizations and Excuses

Possible Rationalization	Challenge to the Rationalization
_____	_____
_____	_____
_____	_____
_____	_____
_____	_____
_____	_____
_____	_____
_____	_____

Exercise 2C: Acting Against Your Rationalizations and Excuses

As you show yourself why your rationalizations and excuses are invalid, also figure out a way to *act* against them, and forcefully push yourself to *take* that action. Thus, when you rationalize, you usually do so to *avoid* taking some uncomfortable or risky action. Figure out what that avoidance is, and make yourself face it and act against it, no matter *how* uncomfortable you feel. The following is a sample worksheet to help you plan and do this.

Sample Practice Sheet for Exercise 2C: Acting Against Your Rationalizations and Excuses

Possible Rationalization	Actions to Overcome This Rationalization
Maybe my son is just going through a phase, and I should just ignore the fact that he's so uncooperative in the morning.	Confront my son; let him know my expectations of him, and why; listen to him but be firm in what I want, and the consequences if not met.
The report isn't really that important. Nobody reads them anyway.	Talk to my boss about how valuable the report really is. Get it done.
My poor performance evaluation is only because I don't play office politics like the others. It has nothing to do with how good a job I'm doing. Everybody couldn't get an excellent rating; I'm just the sacrificial lamb.	Ask someone in the office I trust what they think of my work; talk to the boss about specific areas for improvement, and what has not been getting done satisfactorily, and what his expectations are for a better evaluation; submit a plan of action to the boss as to how I intend to meet the improvements.
My husband had it coming to him. He's not supportive; he always takes their side and criticizes me.	Take responsibility for my behavior in the fight with him (tell him I could be wrong) and *discuss* (not argue again) my concern about wanting more support.

Your Practice Sheet for Exercise 2C: Acting Against Your
Rationalizations and Excuses

Possible Rationalization

Actions to Overcome This
Rationalization

_____   _____

_____   _____

_____   _____

_____   _____

_____   _____

_____   _____

_____   _____

_____   _____

Chapter 3

Realistic Preferences: A Powerful Alternative to the Nutty Thinking We Do That Upsets Us

Awfulizing, shoulding, and rationalizing are three of the main ways in which we allow other people and things to push our buttons to the point where we don't handle difficult situations as effectively as we could. And we make ourselves miserable in the process. By now you may have surmised the major anti-button-pushing strategy we outline in this book: People and things do *not* actually push our buttons. They themselves *seem* to get to us, but in fact the way we think and react *in response to* them is what determines how upset we get, and how we react in specific situations. We push our *own* buttons! And we can learn *not* to push them!

Fortunately, there is a fourth type of thinking we can do at Point B when someone or something either is trying to, or might try to, push our buttons. This type is easy to understand, but difficult to do (especially when someone *is* getting to you). We will show you *how* to do it, but actually *doing* it will take practice, practice, practice. Because all of us are always thinking in *some* way in *every* situation, this anti-button-pushing practice doesn't require a lot of extra time. But we will show you how to systematically choose how you will think in a specific situation, as opposed to what may have come "naturally" in the past.

The fourth type of thinking comes out in the form of *realistic preferences*. The most effective ones are (e.g.): "I want...," "I'd like...," "I'd prefer...," and "It would be better if..." They all sound simple enough, right? Now let us show you their power.

Let's start with a true story from our own experience—since we use these techniques all the time, too. At this point in my career, I (A.L.) have given over 5,000 largely unflustered presentations. But when I was to give my very first talk, I was pretty darn nervous. It was to be in front of several hundred people, and I started my thinking with some great awfulizing: "What if I do a terrible job? What if everyone is bored to death and starts talking among themselves? What if I get asked a question I can't answer? What if nobody shows up? What if they *all* show up?[11] What if I run out of things to say? What if we take a stretch break and everyone but the front row leaves—and the only reason *they* stay is that they didn't see everyone behind them go?"

Then I started shoulding on myself: "I *should* be able to give a talk to a group. I'm an adult person; I shouldn't let this bother me. If I can't do this, mother was right—I'm a turkey: I'll never amount to anything!"

I even slipped a few rationalizations in to cover up my awfulizing and shoulding: "So what? Who cares? Big deal! It doesn't bother me if the audience doesn't like what I have to offer. If they're too stupid to appreciate what I have to say, that's *their* problem!"

Fortunately, I soon came to actually practice what I preached. I substituted the following realistic preferences over and over, each time I found myself awfulizing, shoulding, or rationalizing: "I'd *like*

---

[11]These last two "what ifs" are especially noteworthy because I could make myself miserable if they *do* or if they *don't* show up. It doesn't matter what the A (Activating Event) is, it is how we *think* about it that largely determines how we handle it.

this group to like me and think highly of what I have to say. If they don't, that's *unfortunate*—but it's not *awful* unless I make it so. I *want to* do a good job, and I will put every effort into it—but if I *don't*, that won't be terrible and horrible. I'll regret it and be disappointed and seriously concerned about it—but also committed to finding out how to improve on it. I'd prefer to answer every question brilliantly—but if I don't, I can handle that without shoulding on myself." By saying these realistic preferences to myself, I challenged the nutty thinking I was doing and substituted thoughts that made sense. I didn't try to convince myself with positive affirmations that I *would* do fine, but rather got at the heart of my anxiety: the beliefs that I *had* to do a good job, and that the group *had* to like me. Those were "wants," not "had to's"—*preferences*, not *shoulds*.

The bullseye point here is that if you awfulize, should on yourself, or rationalize, you will get yourself excessively anxious and uptight, and will likely blow the presentation. But if, instead, you think preferences ("I'd *like to* do a good job, but I don't *have to!*"), you will be concerned before you speak, and disappointed if you do blow it— but you won't let the presentation push your buttons. In my case, I was able to reduce my anxiety significantly before and during the talk.

I was still a little nervous, but that didn't interfere at all. I gave the presentation and it went quite well. I did find some things that (if improved on) could make it better next time, but that fact showed me that I was able both to assess my effort quite objectively, and to learn from it. I could not have done these things if I had indulged in awfulizing or shoulding.

Don't go to the extreme of trying to convince yourself that you *don't care* about doing a lousy job. ("I don't care if I blow it. That won't bother me.") That would be a rationalization and a con. Thinking realistic preferences safely falls in the middle of the two dangerous extremes (awfulizing/shoulding and rationalization), enabling you to have healthy, legitimate feelings when previously you would have overreacted.

It's important to recognize that realistic preferences are not at all like the typical "positive thinking" that people sometimes advocate.

Realistic preferences are *not* suggesting that you can or will be successful—that you *can* handle the situation perfectly, or that everything *will* turn out fine. Realistic preferences are saying that it is okay to give "it" a try—even if you might fail, be rejected, or the like.

If the worst *does* happen, you're not going to be indifferent to it (that would be a rationalization), but rather will be able to handle it. Whether you are committed to trying again or doing something else, you don't get on your own case. It's bad enough if you failed or got rejected—should you also be miserable about it? How you choose to think will determine how you handle button-pushers and button-pushing situations alike.

The idea of thinking in terms of realistic preferences instead of demands is incredibly easy to understand. But, again, don't kid yourself—it's often difficult to *do,* especially when someone or something is pushing your buttons. Yes, it takes hard work and persistent effort—but the rewards are great!

The best way to understand and appreciate the power of awfulizing, shoulding, rationalizing, and realistic preferences is to see how differently you tend to *act* when you think each way. Dead ahead are some typical button-pushing situations which people bring up in workshops that we, the authors, give across the United States and in other countries. In each case we will present an example of awfulizing, shoulding, rationalizing, and realistic preferences for a typical button-pushing situation. There are lots of other ways you might react in each particular situation, but these are our choices of examples to show how your thoughts can lead to very different behaviors. (When we describe the thinking, the points in parentheses are the *implied* thoughts that we don't actually think "out loud" but that do underlie our thinking. They help to clarify what is upsetting you.)

"Oh My God, Not Timmy!"

Your 15-year-old son, Tim, has been "different" lately. He is more "into himself" and is exceptionally irritable. He looks tired, and is not always well-focused. Actually, this could be pretty normal for *any* teenager. But then you find marijuana and cocaine in his room. He first denies it's his, and then blows up, claiming it's none of your business what he does, and that "everybody's" been doing it all along.

Possible Awfulizing

"What if he's been doing this right under our noses all along? What if he's addicted? What if he's selling this stuff to others? What if he refuses to stop? What if he runs away? What if he's been stealing, or something worse, to get the money for this stuff? What if we've failed as parents? What if he's already done permanent damage to himself?" (That would be *awful!* I couldn't stand it!)

Possible Shoulding on Others

"He's a disgrace to his family! How dare he do this? After all we've done for him, how could he turn on us like this? They *should* put him in jail and throw away the key. Not only do we catch him, but then he lies and, even worse, defends his lies! He's *got to* be taught a lesson, and a good one!" (He *shouldn't* be doing this; he's *got to* be punished; he *must not* lie or defend it!)

Possible Shoulding on Yourself

"We *should* have been watching him more carefully. We *must* be terrible parents! We *shouldn't* both be working. We've been negligent. We've failed him." (We *ought* to be ashamed of ourselves.)

Possible Behaviors If Awfulizing and Shoulding

Attacking and threatening Tim and having a tremendous fight. "You're disgusting! Look at you, a drug addict! What's in that head of yours, anything at all? Can't you be trusted to do a single thing right? How long have you been deceiving us? How could you do this to us? We've given you everything! Well, you're going to pay for this one! We have a good mind to turn you into the police right now! Where'd you get the money for this garbage? Steal it? From us? We can't even look at you. Get out of our sight!"

Possible Rationalizations

"This just isn't like him. He's such a wonderful child. Someone put him up to this. It's got to be that new friend of his; I knew there was something about him I didn't like. What can we do nowadays to keep him from such bad influences? They're everywhere. I'm sure he really isn't behaving any worse than any of the other kids."

Possible Behaviors If Rationalizing

Scold him for having drugs, and put the blame on his friends. Refuse to let his friends in the house. Warn him that if you ever see anything like this again, there will be big trouble. Worry a lot.

Possible Realistic Preferences

"I am deeply concerned about this. I am shocked that he is involved in drugs. I could easily blow up, but if I do, I'll be part of the problem. I want to talk with Tim about this and find out more about the extent of his involvement. I am committed to doing this in a functional way. I do not have to overreact. I can be very serious without losing control. I want to let him know that I strongly disapprove of this, that I hate what he is doing but do not hate him, and that I care for him very much. I want him to understand that drug use is serious and dangerous. I want him to stop right now."

Possible Behaviors If Thinking Realistic Preferences

You might say to your son: "This is a very serious problem and I want to talk with you about it. I'm sorry that you have used such poor judgment, but I'm also really concerned about how involved you are with drugs. I want you to know I love you even though I deplore your behavior. I want to help you with this."

After talking with him about *why* he's been doing drugs, how often he's been doing it, and what you are going to do to help him stop, it may also be appropriate to penalize him for his behavior. What you do to penalize him depends on so many different factors in each case that it's hard to give any rules. But it's important to know that *some* form of *strong* penalty may be appropriate. Parents can be loving, caring, and concerned, but also be disciplinarians who carry out fair penalties for inappropriate behaviors.

"Not Now, Dear!"

You are feeling very romantic, and in fact sexually turned on. You look over to your spouse, raise an eyebrow, move over next to her, start kissing and touching her. You feel like seducing her. She, however, is not nearly as responsive as you would prefer. (This may be generally true, or she might not be responsive for the moment).

Possible Awfulizing

"Maybe she's not turned on to me. What if she thinks I'm a lousy lover? Maybe I don't satisfy her. (How horrible! That would be *awful!*) What if she's just getting back at me for something? What if she's really not interested in sex anymore? *That* would *really* stink!"

Possible Shoulding

"What's bugging her? Damn it, every time I feel sexy and turned on, she's not interested. She probably *never* liked sex. What a prude! I need somebody who gets excited—that's what turns me on even more. But her, she's just a wet dishrag. Why even bother? She's frigid! She's so uptight she doesn't know *how* to enjoy sex (and she *should*). I know what *she* needs!"

Possible Behaviors If Awfulizing and Shoulding

"What's the matter with you *this* time? Got a headache? You're a real drag, you know that? I'm feeling turned on and I start fooling around, and what do you do? Nothing! You just lie there. You turn me right off. What's the matter, don't you like sex any more? Did you ever? You really know how to make a guy feel good about himself!" (Then storm out, sleep on the couch, sulk for days, go out with the guys.)

Possible Rationalization

"Well, maybe she's tired. We've been pretty busy lately. Maybe I did something wrong. I hope she's not mad at me. Sex isn't everything—maybe she'll snap out of this soon. We all have our moods. I'd better not say anything, or she might *really* get angry."

Possible Behaviors If Thinking Rationalizations

Turn over, not say a word, and lie awake trying to guess what it's all about. Next day, act like nothing happened.

Possible Realistic Preferences

"I'd *like* her to be more responsive than she is, but she doesn't *have to* be. I'm disappointed, but it's not awful that she's not. It may be something about me, or something may be going on with her. Rather than jump to conclusions, take it as an affront to my manhood, or attack her, I can ask her what's going on."

Possible Behaviors If Thinking Realistic Preferences

Ask her, in a genuine and concerned manner, what's going on. If she's honest in return, you will likely have a healthy conversation. If she refuses to talk, or gives really lame excuses (as opposed to valid ones), you have two concerns worthy of discussion: (1) the difference in your sexual interest; and (2) her unwillingness to discuss it. Both are important, but you'd better deal with the latter first. Continuing to try to discuss issues that are being avoided is tough, requiring persistently rational thinking instead of awfulizing and shoulding, or rationalizing to avoid a fight, or just giving up. If you try to talk and she is defensive, *don't* give up—*or* start getting nasty yourself. It's not enough to say, "Well, I tried" if you don't give it a good try often enough. What you are thinking in this situation will influence both *what* you say and *how* you say it. And what you say and how you say it will influence the responses you get from your spouse. Start by focusing your thinking on your realistic preferences.

"Is This Any Way to Run an Airline?"

You have a 9:45 A.M. doctor's appointment for checking out a suspected flu bug. You arrive promptly and proceed to sit in a noisy waiting room (shared jointly by three doctors) for over an hour while others, who came in after you, have long since gotten in and left. When you inquire at the desk, the receptionist indifferently explains that "Doctor" always books two people for every time slot, because "sometimes" one doesn't show up. Today *everyone* did. When you finally do get in, the doctor spends three minutes verifying what you already know, and confirms that "It's really going around town lately." He writes a prescription for a $40 antibiotic (which he says probably won't kill the virus) and charges you $55 for the visit. You usually are expected to pay on your way out—no waiting required.

Possible Awfulizing

In the waiting room: "What if they forgot me? What if they've been putting people ahead of me? What if my doctor isn't even back there? What if I have to sit here all morning?" (That would be *terrible!* I hate these places! I can't stand how they treat people!)

Possible Shoulding

After the appointment: "How do you like that: $55 for nothing! I'm telling you, this is incredible! This ought to be against the law. Somebody's got to do something about this! People should *never* have to wait over an hour for an appointment. They *shouldn't* be allowed to overbook. But we patients are just like lambs. We do anything they say. We treat doctors like gods. I think this is outrageous! He *should* be ashamed to run a business like this and rip people off at the same time. But they don't care—all they want is the money. What ever happened to Marcus Welby? Well, I'm going to give that doctor a piece of my mind!"

Possible Behaviors If Awfulizing and Shoulding

Take it out on the nurse/receptionist (especially since she was so indifferent in the first place): "I don't know how you keep any patients at all, the way you run this office. I've had to wait over an hour for three minutes of nothing. Is that worth $55? *I* certainly don't think so. This is highway robbery! All you care about is money. What ever happened to concern for the patient? Well, you've seen the last of me! Maybe if enough people get smart, they won't tolerate such unprofessional behavior. (Then storm out indignantly.)

Possible Rationalizations

"Maybe the doctor had an emergency. Some patients do take longer than others. I guess they have to make sure they're fully booked; it's probably expensive to run an office like this. I'd probably do the same thing myself, if I were in the doctor's shoes. I just got caught on a bad day, unlucky me."

Possible Behaviors If Rationalizing

Wait and wait and wait. If you do ask at all about when you're "on," do so meekly, as if you're sorry to interrupt the receptionist. Say nothing later—just pay your bill, and leave. (Then gripe about it to everyone in sight.)

Possible Realistic Preferences

"I wanted to get in to see the doctor much more promptly, but I don't *need* to get myself all worked up. I understand that emergencies arise, but that's not the case here and I want something to be done to change this system. I want to express my concern about their booking policy, the delay, and the fee. It's not awful and terrible that this has happened, but it *is* a real inconvenience, and I want to let them know that."

Possible Behaviors If Thinking Realistic Preferences

Expressing your legitimate concerns and frustrations assertively (but not aggressively) to the receptionist and/or the doctor: "When you double-book and everyone does show up, patients—myself included—wind up being seriously inconvenienced by long delays and wasted time, and that's very frustrating." "When I see the doctor for only three or four minutes and I'm charged $55, I believe that's an unreasonable fee. I'd like you to consider a reduced fee for a very brief, uncomplicated visit."

Depending on the response you get, you might ask for a day of non–double booking, or you might choose to go to another doctor (if you can find one who doesn't do the same thing). The difference between this response and the one you were creating by awfulizing and shoulding is that in this case you kept your cool and *still* asserted yourself. If you were awfulizing and shoulding, it might have felt good to get things off your chest—but you let them push your buttons unnecessarily, and they got to you.

Attilla the Boss

You work hard every day, always willing to put out an extra effort— to go the extra mile—to get the job done. Your boss, however, rarely expresses his appreciation, nor does he recognize your extra efforts. On the other hand, he is quick to point out mistakes, can be highly critical before he has all the facts, and is very willing to delegate extra work. You enjoy your work, but you are getting sick and tired of hearing little that's positive and appreciative, and lots that's negative or indifferent.

Possible Awfulizing

"What if I *am* just doing a mediocre job? What if I just keep working harder and getting nothing in return? What if he just doesn't care, or maybe he has it in for me? It really ticks me off that I work as hard as I do, and get no appreciation at all. I'm not a machine. Why can't he just balance the criticisms out occasionally with a positive comment?"

Possible Shoulding

"What a lousy manager I've got! He's got to understand the simple fact that people need some encouragement every now and then to keep them going. Why should I bust my butt trying to do a good job when all I do is get criticized? He needs to learn about people, that creep! I ought to just quit and leave him hanging! *Then* he'd realize what I do. I've got to stand up to that louse and tell him off—I won't be a wimp anymore!"

Possible Behaviors If Awfulizing and Shoulding

Slowing down your efforts; sulking, being less positive toward your boss; being sarcastic or indirectly complaining; getting into arguments with him over other things; complaining to others; making faces behind his back as he leaves your office.

Possible Rationalizing

"It's probably like this everywhere. Bosses are all alike. Maybe if I try harder he'll notice my efforts. Probably not. I'll just do my job, collect my paycheck, and hit the door—but won't expect anything extra. I don't care anymore. The heck with it."

Possible Behaviors If Rationalizing

Withdrawing; losing your morale; being less productive but keeping it all to yourself and saying nothing.

Possible Realistic Preferences

I'd like my boss to appreicate my efforts more, but that doesn't mean he *has* to. I'd prefer that he say some positive things, as well as the criticisms. I'd like him to respect my work and to let me know that he does. If he doesn't improve, I'll regret that. I'm seriously concerned—and I'm committed to doing what I can about this, including talking with him without sounding whiny, defensive, or negative.

Possible Behaviors If Thinking Realistic Preferences

Keeping up your own pride and enthusiasm; maintaining a high level of effort and performance; developing a support system where-with colleagues *can* recognize and appreciate each other; and asking the boss in an appropriate manner to balance his valid criticisms with some positive comments about your efforts. Whether the boss improves or not, you will have handled the situation well—and you didn't let him bug you.

Do you see how very different your behavior can be, depending on how you *think* about your situation? As of this writing, we've been teaching (and practicing) these techniques for a combined 56 years, and are still amazed by the good results. If *you* use them, you can direct and control *how you feel and act in a situation* by directing and controlling *how you think at Point B*. It's not easy, and it takes lots of practice—but it's so well worth it!

EXERCISES

Exercise 3A: Realistic Preferences

Whenever you vigorously (not rigidly!) stay with a realistic preference, you will have a difficult time letting anybody or any situation
push your buttons. Because a realistic preference, wish, or desire
always has an overt or implied *but* in it. Yes, no matter how strong
your preference is! For when you *only* tell yourself, "I'd *like* my boss
or coworker to treat me well," you imply, "*but* he or she doesn't *have*
to. It won't kill me if that person doesn't. I can *still* handle things."

Whenever you feel quite upset, therefore, and let some person or
thing push your buttons, assume that you have *both* a legitimate,
realistic preference *and* an illegitimate, commanding *must, should,*
or *ought.* Persist in finding it, dispute it, and change it back to *only* a
desire or preference.

Here are some examples of changing shoulds and musts to realistic
preferences.

Sample Practice Sheet for Exercise 3A: Realistic Preferences

My Recent Shoulds/Musts	Realistic Preferences I Can Use Instead of These Shoulds/Musts
Maybe my son is just going through a phase, and I should just ignore that he's so uncooperative in the morning.	I'd *like* my son to be cooperative in the morning. I *want* to talk with him about it firmly without blowing up.
This report isn't really that important. Nobody reads them, anyway. I *shouldn't* have to do it!	I'd *prefer* not to do this report but the boss does want it. I'd *like* to convince him of this and if I don't, I will get it done promptly.
My poor performance evaluation is only because I don't play office politics like the others. It has nothing to do with how good a job I'm doing. Everybody couldn't get an excellent rating; I'm just the sacrificial lamb— and I shouldn't be!	I'd *like* to believe that my poor evaluation is only politics but *it would be better* if I asked someone I trust and my boss for specific feedback and get to work on improvements.

My husband had it coming to him. He's not supportive; he always takes their side and criticizes me. He *must* not be so critical!

I *want* my husband to be less critical and more supportive but I do not have to fight with him about that. I'd *prefer* to *discuss* it with him without being defensive.

Your Practice Sheet for Exercise 3A: Realistic Preferences

My Recent Shoulds/Musts

Realistic Preferences I Can Use Instead of These Shoulds/Musts

_____   _____
_____   _____
_____   _____
_____   _____
_____   _____
_____   _____
_____   _____
_____   _____
_____   _____

Exercise 3B: Using Rational-Emotive Imagery to Achieve Realistic Preferences

Rational emotive imagery is an emotive exercise created by Dr. Maxie C. Maultsby, Jr. in 1971. In our version, you imagine one of the worst things that could happen to you—such as failing in an important project and being severely criticized therefor by your boss or supervisor. Let yourself feel very upset about this (excessively anxious, angry, depressed, or guilty), and get in touch with this feeling and really, really *experience* it. Then make a strong effort to *change* this feeling to a quite *appropriate* or *preferential* one—such as keen disappointment and regret, but *not* anxiety or depression.

You can just about always change your *in*appropriate negative feelings to *appropriate* negative emotions (at Point C) when you imagine something unfortunate happening to you (at Point A). *You* create and control your feelings. To make yourself anxious or depressed, you tell yourself something like, "I *must* not fail on this project! They can't criticize me! This is a disaster. I'm all washed up. I *am* a failure! And they know it!" So, to make yourself (yes, *make* yourself) feel, instead, appropriately disappointed or regretful, you can change your demands to *preferences*, such as: "I'd *like* to succeed at this project and have my boss or supervisor respect me, *but* if I fail and get rejected, my life won't end. I can handle it, and I can still be involved and enthusiastic about my work, in spite of this misfortune." If you think this *preferential* way, and really *believe* what you are telling yourself, you'll almost always begin to feel appropriate feelings. And if you repeat this kind of rational-emotive imagery every day for about a month, you'll *automatically* begin to think and feel *preferentially* rather than *mustingly* when you think of adverse Activating Events (A), or actually encounter them.

To employ rational-emotive imagery (REI) you can refer to the following sample practice sheet, and then fill out one of your own.

Sample Practice Sheet for Exercise 3B: Using Rational-Emotive Imagery to Achieve Realistic Preferences

Unfortunate Event Vividly Imagined	Emotional Overreactions I Can Produce by Vividly Imaging This Event	Alternative Desired Feelings	Thoughts I Can Use to Produce the Desired Feelings
My son is uncooperative in the morning when we are getting ready for school and work.	Enraged; furious.	Frustrated, seriously concerned.	I *want* him to cooperate, but he doesn't deserve my wrath if he doesn't. It *would be better if* I talk to him calmly and firmly without blowing up. I can handle this without a fight.
Not having the report ready for the boss.	Excessive anxiety and defensiveness.	Disappointed, and committed to completing it.	*It would have been better* if I had completed the report on time. I didn't, and, rather than justifying it, I want to take responsibility for getting it done promptly. I can accept and handle the boss's disapproval.
Getting a poor performance evaluation.	Shock; denial; extreme anxiety.	Seriously concerned and accepting.	I'd *like* to have gotten a better evaluation, but I didn't—and I can live with that without finding excuses. I'd *like* to learn what I can do to improve and get working on it.

| Having a fight with my husband after a rotten day. | Totally fed up; irate. | Frustrated and regretful. | I *want* my husband to be more supportive, and I can talk with him about that without blowing up. We can be close to each other, even if he doesn't respond as I'd *like* him to. I can admit my part in this fight. |

Your Practice Sheet for Exercise 3B: Using Rational-Emotive Imagery to Achieve Realistic Preferences

Unfortunate Event Vividly Imagined	Emotional Overreactions I Can Produce by Vividly Imaging This Event	Alternative Desired Feelings	Thoughts I Can Use to Produce the Desired Feelings

Chapter 4

Ten Nutty Beliefs That We Use to Let People and Situations Needlessly Push Our Buttons

In 1956, I (A.E.) identified ten screwball beliefs that can lead us to push our own buttons in specific situations. That's quite a few but, in fact, the first four alone account for the great majority of our overreactions to people and events. These are nutty beliefs that we often awfulize, should, and rationalize *about* in specific situations. They are the underlying screwball foundations that each of us carries around to one degree or another. We will show you how to identify these irrational beliefs, how they are influencing your reactions in a specific situation and, most importantly, how to keep them from contributing to your overreactions.

The first screwball belief that people often tend to awfulize, should, and rationalize about is:

Irrational Belief No. 1: *worrying too much about what other people think of you*. Excess worrying creates a strong fear of rejection. The underlying thought goes something like "I *must not* be disapproved of or rejected by significant people in my life (relatives, friends, bosses, coworkers, teachers, etc.), because if I were it would be *awful* and I *couldn't stand it*. Now, very few people would say, "Yes, I have thought those exact words many times!" We generally don't think that specifically. But *it is* the underlying *general belief* that comes out in the form of specific awfulizing, shoulding, and rationalizations in specific situations or with specific people in our lives.

If you hold this irrational belief, you may easily behave in one of two main dysfunctional ways. First, you may run around trying terribly hard to please everyone, avoiding conflicts and getting others to like you even if it means ignoring what *you* want or think. Edith Bunker, Archie's dizzily beleaguered wife in "All in the Family," was a great example. She tried *so* hard to please: "Oh, you better stop talking about that—Archie's coming home soon, and *he* might get *upset*." "Don't sit in *that* chair; that's *Archie's* chair." "We're having this for dinner again 'cause *Archie likes it*."

Very few people walk around actually thinking: "I am too worried about what others think of me." But in a specific situation, like when the boss is criticizing you in front of your peers, or you're being put on the spot when asked a question in a meeting, or you're being rejected by your spouse, or you are meeting new people, or on a first date, you can immediately worry too much about what others think of you.

Many people expend enormous energies trying to get others to like or respect them. They avoid expressing opinions that someone might not agree with. They bend over backwards trying to please. They change their positions like chameleons change their color and "go with the flow." In their personal lives they worry whether they are liked, loved, popular, accepted, attractive, impressive, as good as, "in," or "up with the Joneses." We sometimes call them "overly sensitive" or "thin-skinned."

That's not to say that you shouldn't care at all about what other people think of you. That would be a rationalization. Not to care at all would be a con, almost sociopathic. Yet we, the authors of this book, have both often seen spouses terribly afraid of what their mate might think if they spoke up, or took a position on some issue, or expressed a preference that might be counter to the spouse's. We have also seen parents raise brats spoiled because mom and dad were afraid the child would be upset if they took a firm stand or—Heaven forbid—said no. (And they're still treating those kids that way when the brats are 30). We've seen salespeople manipulate customers into buying something more expensive than they could really afford because the salesperson insinuated that they couldn't afford it, and they had to prove they could. We've seen people go deeply into debt to impress friends and neighbors with cars, homes, furnishings, clothes, spas, and other accoutrements of the good life. All of these people let someone or something push their buttons. Other people hide in corners and make themselves miserable (but safe) at parties and other social events, for fear that they might have to talk with someone and be rejected, or make a fool of themselves. The sufferer calls that problem "shyness." Some "experts" say the person has "low self-esteem," as though that explains it. But it simply describes it. The *cause* is mainly the awfulizing, shoulding, and rationalizing done due to worrying too much about what others think of you. And you can *change* that thinking.

On the job it's a little different, but essentially the same issue. You usually don't care if everyone "likes" you on the job. That's nice, but it's not essential. You don't have to go bowling, or to dinner and the theater on weekends, with your colleagues or bosses. But on the job many people worry *too much* about their image and how they are perceived. As Rodney Dangerfield puts it, "I don't get no *respect!*" In our training workshops with organizations, we've seen people make themselves miserable because they weren't praised enough by their colleagues or bosses. We've seen managers in staff meetings sit silent, even though they had great ideas, because they were afraid they would be criticized, ridiculed, or otherwise jumped on. We've seen supervisees let their bosses treat them demeaningly, or pile the work on ad nauseum, and not say a reasonable word because that might make the boss angry. Then they quit, and the insensitive boss never even knows why. Some people worry so much about what the boss might think that they don't think for themselves. They play it safe and cover themselves by becoming "Yes, boss" clones—or they spend more time trying to get recognition by playing office politics. Others see putdowns and affronts at every meeting, in every glance and tone, in every decision. They often feel victimized and very sorry for themselves. Image becomes more important than substance.

There is a second way some people deal with fear of rejection. It appears to be the exact opposite of worrying too much about what others think of you, but is precisely the same. We think Edith is the Bunker who is overworried or insecure. But what about Archie? He just hides behind his wall (or bunker) and then, every time he is challenged or someone disagrees, he attacks with such blasts as "Stifle yourself, Dingbat!" and "Hey, Meathead—is that another dumb idea out of your books?" According to Archie, the best defense against rejection is a good offense: Get the others before they get you.

Some attackers hide their insecurity by being subtler. They are quietly disapproving, superior, distant, judgmental, sarcastic, negative, and/or condescending toward people who may not approve of them. They hold everyone at arm's length, or further. Their goal is to keep others off balance in order to protect their own fragile egos. They are just as afraid of what other people think of them, but they hide behind a wall. Another type in this defensive category simply withdraws into a shell. They don't attack—they pull into their bunkers and don't let anyone get close. They are distant and detached. They tend to have few friends, and sometimes convince themselves that they *prefer* to be loners.

Instead of awfulizing, shoulding, and rationalizing about what others think of you, you can teach yourself to think *realistic preferences.* "I'd like people to like me. Especially if they're people I care for a lot. If they do, great! If they don't, I regret it—it's unfortunate. I am genuinely concerned, and I am committed to doing what I can (and what I'm *willing* to do) to improve their reaction. If I really can't do anything, or I choose not to, then I *accept* that these people are not going to like or respect me. I still take *responsibility* for my actions, and I will not use that as an excuse to say 'That's your problem, not mine.' *That* would be a rationalization."

Your realistic preferences (*those that you would think to yourself*) could also go like this: "I'd like you to like and respect me, but if you won't, that's not awful, terrible, or horrible, and I *can* stand it. I am seriously concerned, because I think our relationship is important, and I am *committed* to doing everything I can to make it better. But I am not going to make myself miserable trying to win your approval, liking, love, or respect. If I do get rejected, then I have two choices: (1) I can *accept* that you do not like, love, or respect me; or (2) I can leave and/or find relationships wherein I *can* get my wants met."

Throughout this book we will attack the crazy idea that you *must* have the approval, liking, love, or respect of others. Successfully challenging the inclination to give other people so much power and importance will go a *long* way toward not letting them push your buttons!

The second main nutty belief that I (A.E.) described at the annual convention of the American Psychological Association in Chicago in 1956, leads to excessive *fear of failure:*

Irrational Belief No. 2: *"I must not fail at important tasks* [in business, school, sports, sex, relationships, etc.], *and if I do it's terrible and I can't stand it."* Simply stated, it's worrying *too much* about screwing up. If you have convinced yourself that it is not OK to fail at anything important, and you run into a situation where you might fail, you'll either avoid that situation at all costs or, if you can't get out of it, probably fulfill your prophesy that you *will* fail. You certainly won't be thinking as clearly as you could!

There are dramatic examples of fear of failure: A number of wealthy moguls committed suicide during the Depression. An athlete who had never lost a race was losing badly, ran off the course, and jumped off a bridge. Gifted high-school students who narrowly miss a 4.0 grade-point average, and undergraduates who fail to be admitted to medical school, at times attempt suicide. A politician gets embroiled in a scandal or controversy, and contracts a serious degenerative illness.

Certainly these are extreme cases and do not often touch our own lives directly—but they happen all too often. We more frequently get overly anxious when we encounter situations like job interviews, meeting new people, career changes, ending relationships, speaking up in meetings, or trying things we may not be "good" at.

Fear of failure often leads to a lack of risk-taking, which leads to stagnation, which leads to mediocrity. Sometimes we get so set in our ways that we refuse to think or act in new or different ones. That seems just plain rigid, but often it's more a result of being overly afraid to try something new because it might not work out, or might make us look bad. The perfectionists are the real extremists. They actually *believe* that they must be perfect at everything they undertake, and this miscalculation causes them either to not even try, or to fail to finish because of "not being good enough." They often have dozens of unfinished projects lying around.

Fear of failure can keep you from even considering new possibilities, ideas, curiosities, directions, goals, and innovations. If you think about them, then you of course have to face the possibility that you *might* fail. You then certainly won't talk about them, or, perish the thought, actually pursue them! The worst part of downing yourself when you fail is not the failures themselves, but the many things you never even *try*. It's the loss (or absence) of so many interesting experiences that you never get to appreciate. Exceptional people have long since realized that they learn as much from their failures as from their successes—or more.

One of the best examples of an absence of fear of failure was the late Richard Feynman. Not exactly a household name, but he won a Nobel Prize in physics and was on the *Challenger* space-shuttle disaster investigation team. Not bad! But it's his attitude (almost a philosophy of life) that impressed. He would try anything, and was insatiably curious. Aside from his specialization in physics he was an artist, played street music in Brazil and became an expert safe-cracker! He simply believed that it was OK to try things he *wasn't* sure he could do. He was willing to try and possibly *fail*. It never occurred to him to avoid something because he might not be good at it.

Someone once said, "If you are hitting the bullseye every time you shoot, you are standing too close!" Stretching ourselves beyond what we already know we can do includes failing sometimes—and that's OK! A great poem expresses this point:

> Sometimes it tends to drive me hazy—
> Am I, or are the others, crazy?
> —Albert Einstein

Even *Einstein* wondered if he was nuts to challenge the basic theories of gravity accepted by his colleagues—to explain the unexplained. Thank goodness he didn't have a fear of failure! Thank goodness he didn't let others push his buttons to the point where he abandoned his position for fear of being ostracized!

Another result of excessive fear of failure is often the inability to stand criticism. Some people have excuses, justifications, defenses, and counterattacks for everything. They let others push their buttons because they cannot tolerate the possibility of being wrong. Their defensiveness can leap out over tiny, insignificant matters (food preferences, opinions about TV shows, how to fix the squeaky door) or more important issues (business decisions, buying a house, drinking habits). The basis of their defensiveness is avoiding the possibility of being wrong or a failure. Believing that it is totally unacceptable to be wrong or to fail leaves you wide open for others to push your buttons.

The third screwball belief that we awfulize, should, and rationalize about is often LFT (Low Frustration Tolerance). It goes something like this:

Irrational Belief No. 3: *"People and things should always turn out the way I want them to—and if they don't it's awful, terrible, and horrible, and I can't stand it!"* Some people talk to themselves like this all the time: "I can't stand it when he/she always...," or "It drives me crazy when the...," or "I just hate it and can't bear it whenever...." They literally talk themselves into unnecessary upsets.

At times, little things can bug you just as much as big things. Often even more than the biggies. Sometimes it's a tone of voice, or a look on someone's face, or static on the phone, or the mail is late, or the line is long, or the salesperson was snotty, or the traffic was heavy, or.... With things that are *very* important, it's a pushover to make ourselves overly upset. A sudden change in a deadline, or an equipment breakdown, can really get to you. The "upsetness" doesn't make the problem go away or solve anything (as a matter of fact, you probably make poorer decisions, and deal with others less effectively), but you don't question your reaction because it seems so *natural*.

Now, it *is* natural to "get" very upset and agitated when things aren't going as you would like. But is *natural* necessarily always good for you? No! It most assuredly does feel good—temporarily—to get things off your chest, but that rarely helps solve problems that won't go away (just because you blew up), and indeed it often makes them worse. An alternative is *not* to hold these feelings inside, but rather to *attack* them and *reduce* them to a level that enables you to handle the situation more functionally.

Thomas Edison screwed up on his light-bulb experiments almost 800 times before he lit (pun intended!) on a winner. Thank goodness he didn't have excessive fear of failure, or low frustration tolerance! I (A.L.) used to say that if he had quit prematurely, we'd all be out on the lawn, or working by candlelight—but that's not true at all. Somebody else, who did *not* have a fear of failure, or low frustration tolerance, would have figured it out.

Teenagers come first to mind when we think of low frustration tolerance. So many kids have a short fuse as soon as things are not going in their desired direction. They often quickly upset themselves about their parents and their "stupid" decisions. "I can't *stand* it when you treat me like a child!" Many seem to have little tolerance for failure in others as well as in themselves. Some deal with their own failure by means of denial and rationalization ("That's a dumb sport, anyway" and "The teacher was a jerk"). Others upset themselves by shoulding on parents, brothers, sisters, and various others for their own failures. For some teens, if they try out for a sport and don't make the first team, they quit right away. If they take a class in an area that's new, and do poorly on the first paper or test, they drop the class. They could turn out to be like so many of us who have never developed the qualities of tenacity, diligence, and perseverance—all worth developing *and* all directly related to our thinking.

Low frustration tolerance is by no means restricted to adolescents, however. Does it affect you? Do you let things, big and little, get to you? Such things as not getting the hoped-for promotion or raise; waiting for the delivery person who doesn't show up as promised; having the boss take credit for your work; fighting when your spouse has not been as attentive as you would like; or finding that the directions for putting together your new purchase are all screwed up, and some of the parts are missing.

If you quickly make yourself overly upset about these things by awfulizing and shoulding, you will soon be part of the problem. Again, your appropriate alternative is not to roll over and say "So what? Who cares?" but rather to think in terms of preferences: "I'd *like* to figure these directions out quickly, but it may take some time." or "I'd *prefer* to have been given the promotion or raise." or "It *would be better* if the boss gave me due credit where it is due." or "I *want* my spouse to be more attentive—but it's not happening, and I regret it. I'm disappointed, seriously concerned, and *committed* to doing everything I can to correct this situation."

There is a corollary that often goes along with the belief that things should always turn out the way the individual wants them to: "I should always be treated *fairly* all the time." Now, you can almost laugh at the absurdity of that idea—but in fact don't you often feel very upset when you believe you've been treated unfairly? When I (A.L.) ask audiences, "How many people here believe the world is fair?" nobody ever raises a hand (except perhaps one or two psychotic people). We *know* the world is not fair, yet we still get overly upset when it's unfair to *us*. We start thinking, very early on, that the world should be fair to us *in particular*.

Sometimes I think that little children's first three learned responses are "Mama," "Dada," and "That's not *fair!*" *Nothing* that parents, or brothers and sisters, do is fair. But learning (and accepting) that the world is *not* always fair is a great and valuable discovery! We genuinely believe that if you treat others directly, they will probably treat you decently in return. But sometimes you go the extra mile, reach out, make the extra effort, and they still take advantage of you.

Now, we're *not* suggesting that you stop treating people decently. We're saying *don't* stop—but *don't* be stunned and get overly upset if they don't reciprocate. There are some "bad actors" in this world— people who frequently are selfish, insensitive, self-centered, and otherwise thoughtless. Sometimes we get terribly bent out of shape when someone treats us insensitively, manipulates us, exploits us, takes advantage, or is downright unfair. Therefore, we are *not* suggesting that if you are treated unfairly, you roll over and say "Hit me again, baby. Beat me to a pulp" or "Well—ha, ha—nobody's perfect. Maybe they didn't mean it." You can still decide to *do* everything possible to redress injustices and unfairnesses, whether they be personal or social, *without overreacting and becoming part of the problem.*

Sometimes low frustration tolerance and awfulizing about unfairness leave us feeling helpless and victimized (as a victim of others and/or of circumstances). There's always a "they" or an "it" keeping us from being something (happier, more successful, promoted, wealthier, more interesting, popular). "If my boss wasn't so intimidated by my capabilities, I'd have been promoted long ago." "If those neighbors weren't so snooty, we'd get along fine." "If my teachers weren't so boring, I'd get good grades." "If the economy hadn't changed, I'd be a millionaire."

There may be a grain of truth to these "if only's," but the real message is, "Through no fault of my own, things have not worked out." Consequently, people who think that things should always turn out the way they want, and that they themselves should always be treated fairly, can easily become whiners. They then will complain about everything and everybody else. If they're lucky, they find another person who thinks the same way—and they can gripe together. And if they really hit the jackpot (on the job, in the neighborhood, or in the family), they find *several* people who regularly feel victimized, and have a *group gripe.* This complaining, however, contributes little to the resolution of any problems or concerns. Admittedly it's natural, but it just doesn't do much good.

You can see, then, that LFT and upsetness about unfairnesses can lead to impulsive reactions, premature quitting, negativism, avoidance of responsibility, victimization, whining, feeling sorry for yourself, helplessness, petty jealousy, and *lack of perseverance.*

I (A.L.) have often wondered why so many employers require MBA degrees of their employees. Very often the same employers complain about how the classroom is not the real world—yet they want their people to have that degree.

After twenty-five years in academia, I have come to the conclusion that the people who have attained masters and doctoral degrees are not necessarily more intelligent (but maybe more knowledgeable in the applied fields, like business) than the non-degreed. Admittedly, there is a certain amount of intellectual capability required to perform at each level of academia, but there are ten times as many people without letters after their names who are just as intelligent as those who have them.

One quality that *is* really valuable in these degreed people, however, is *perseverance.* The degreed people took on a major task, systematically stuck to it, and persevered until it was completed. They took all those classes—many of which were not intrinsically thrilling. They wrote all those papers, studied for all the exams, and did all their research. That's the kind of diligent effort valued in business even though it may have less to do with the content learned. The attitudes learned and the systematic efforts practiced are evidence of their capacity for commitment. There was no place for LFT and upsetness over unfairnesses in such an undertaking. That's not to say that getting an academic degree is the only way to demonstrate perseverance—there's an endless number of ways! But getting rid of LFT is a very important step toward systematically accomplishing *any* major undertaking.

A fourth screwball belief goes like this:

Irrational Belief No. 4: *"If any of the first three bad events happens* (if I'm not liked or respected, if I fail, or if things don't turn out as I'd like—or at least fairly], *then I'll always blame someone for it! They acted wrongly, as they should not have done, and they are rotten people for acting in that terrible way!"*

Many people are excellent at focusing on who's to blame when a problem arises. You can often distinguish functional groups from dysfunctional ones in as quickly as a single meeting. In the *dysfunctional* groups, when the first problem arises, 80 percent of the time is spent on who is to blame for its occurrence, and a mere 20 percent on what to do about it. In the *functional* groups, 80 percent of the time is spent on what to do about it, and *no time* is spent on who is to blame. Rather, the first 20 percent is devoted to identifying who is responsible for both this problem *and* its solution.

Responsibility is different from blame! Have you ever worked in a situation where it was OK to say, in a meeting, "Yes, I am responsible for this problem area [or this aspect of the problem]?" And nobody immediately chopped off your head? Where it was OK to accept responsibility, and then proceed to focus on what to do about it?

We have seen so many organizations where the name of the game is CYA. You know the CYA philosophy of management, don't you? "Cover Your Flanks." (We know Flanks doesn't start with an A, but it's close enough.) Everyone in a meeting is insinuating (or downright saying) that the "real" problem rests with some other department or person. Production blames engineering, which blames research and development, which blames marketing, which blames sales, which blames finance and accounts receivable. The grenade gets lobbed all around the room. You know who usually winds up being fragged? Whoever didn't show up at the meeting!

Some organizations do this kind of hot-potato routine by levels, rather than across departments or different shifts. Supervisors blame the unions for poor productivity because "they" back the bosses when the honchos confront poor work performance. Front-line managers blame middle management for not backing their efforts at accountability. Middle management says that it's the executives who don't care about accountability—"they" are too busy with their heads in the clouds, and don't want to be bothered. Top divisional executives blame corporate executives—and the corporate executives blame the unions! It all goes full circle, and the problems remain.

When there are personality clashes in an office, it's always someone else who is to blame. There is ample evidence to prove who's at fault, and it's gossiped all over the office. The only problem is that *both* people are doing the spreading (sometimes with a little exaggeration or reinterpretation).

Some of us do the same things at home. One spouse testily asks, "Why do you *always*...?" (You can fill in your own endings.) The other spouse replies defensively, "Well, I wouldn't always...if you weren't such a..." Whereupon the original grenade lobber says, "I wouldn't be such a "deedle-dee" if you weren't such a "dum-de-dum." This couple is once again off and running, blaming each other and exchanging verbal blows. The thing that starts it all often is so small that neither person can easily remember the next day what it was— but they both remember all too well the nasty exchanges that were hurled back and forth.

Whether in work or in our personal lives, we can create an atmosphere, a climate, a prevailing attitude where it is OK to take responsibility for our own actions without feeling like we have to play CYA or be defensive. People who have to blame others typically are people who are overly worried about what others think of them, or who fear failure so much that they cannot take responsibility. They have to blame others instead.

Some people have a strong tendency to direct the blame inward, onto themselves. They *should* on themselves regularly for every slight imperfection or failure. They are overly self-critical, and usually finish by feeling lousy about themselves. They wind up either giving up or being very bitter and withdrawn. People who should on themselves and others are living life at about 30 percent and are miserable. Taking responsibility is healthy; constantly blaming oneself is like nourishing a cancer.

Your other main self-defeating, nutty beliefs (numbers 5 through 10) do not manifest themselves as often as the Big Four, but they can be just as disruptive in a specific situation:

Irrational Belief No. 5: *"If I worry obsessively about some upcoming event or how someone really feels about me, things will actually turn out better."* If you stop and think about it, you know that all that worrying in advance didn't do a thing to help you meet the deadline, pay your bills, get the job, or make your in-laws' visit any more enjoyable. Yet you may persist in dwelling on all the "what ifs" and "shoulds" that make you miserable, sometimes for weeks in advance.

Irrational Belief No. 6: *"Perfect solutions exist for every problem, and I must find them—and immediately!"* If you wait for perfect solutions you often will miss the whole trip. Sometimes we tie ourselves up in knots of indecision because every alternative has some negative aspects: "Should I marry him/her or not?" "Should I quit, or stay on the job?" "Should I buy this house, or that one—or just keep renting?" "Should I go on this trip, or not?" "Should I speak up, or not?"

Searching for perfect solutions often will lead to stagnation and frustration. Perseverance, tolerance for less than perfection (but striving for it), the pursuit of improvement, and commitment to doing the very best you can, all are healthy, and most likely to yield the best results. Eliminating unreasonable demands for perfect solutions in no way reduces your commitment to doing or being the very best you *can* do or be. *Wanting* to find perfect solutions and tenaciously pursuing the very best in yourself is very different from awfulizing and shoulding when the perfect solution is not readily available or apparent.

Irrational Belief No. 7: *"It is easier to avoid difficult situations and responsibilities than to face them."* This is one of the most disruptive rationalizations of all. We can literally talk ourselves out of almost anything, yet make it sound believable!

Once there was a revivalist preacher who would go on for hours about the evils of demon rum and alcohol. About halfway through his sermon he used a gimmick to make his point. He would hold up a glass with water in it and another glass with alcohol in it and drop a worm in each. Then he'd put them down on a table in full view and go on with his sermon. A few minutes later he returned to the glasses, held them up and shouted, "See! See what I'm saying to you!" and sure enough the worm in the water was wiggling frantically while the worm in the alcohol was dead as a doornail. Again, he exclaimed "Do you see the point?" And a drunkard who had wandered in at the rear shouted back, "Yeah, if I drink lots of booze I ain't never gonna have worms!" We can make anything fit what we want it to fit especially to avoid facing something difficult.

"It's not the right time to ask for a raise. It just wouldn't do any good anyway." "She never listens to me." "I'm not good at this, why don't you make the call." "It won't work here." "Well, maybe he didn't really mean it." "What do you want me to do, just walk up to him and say, 'Hi, my name's Sue, how do you like me so far?'" There is often some truth to rationalizations but they are designed to keep us from feeling guilty about whatever it is we just avoided.

Irrational Belief No. 8: *"If I never get seriously involved in anything, and maintain a detached perspective, I will never be unhappy."* This is a doozy of a rationalization, too. We know that it sounds nutty (maybe even confusing)—but haven't you ever seen people in meetings at work, or on committees, with their family, who are constantly opposed to everything? They are always outside the tent, shooting in. They don't even get excited about their own criticisms! Why did they ever get into the meeting, or onto the committee, in the first place? They have a "Yes, *but...*" for everything, and a reason why nothing will work, or why they can't help. They remind us of Morris, the cat on those TV commercials, who can't even get interested in mice! Everything is wrong with society—parents, the job, the proposed plan, other people's ideas, the boss, the spouse, and the neighbors—but *they* don't get in an uproar about it. They just sit there and passively make observations. If you seek their opinion or preference they'll say, "Oh, I don't care." But they really think, "Just make sure I like it"—a condition which rarely is met.

The bottom line is that if they *did* get involved they might not be very good at it (*whatever* the "it" is), so they stay detached and passive. Mentally dropping out clearly does not lead to happiness. It's admittedly safer—but not very stimulating or rewarding.

Screwball beliefs 9 and 10 both seek to abdicate by explaining away any responsibility for feelings and actions:

Irrational Belief No. 9: *"It was my past and all the awful things that happened to me when I was a child, or in my last relationship, or in my last job, that causes me to feel and act this way now."* Examples: "My parents were alcoholics." "I was an only child." "I didn't do well in school." "I had a horrible adolescence." "I have low self-esteem because I wasn't toilet-trained properly." "My ex-husband verbally abused me." "I was teased a lot in high school."

There is no question that our past experiences have the *potential* to influence greatly our present behavior, *if we let them.* If, when we focus on the past, we awfulize or should on ourselves or rationalize, these thoughts will increase the potential to make ourselves excessively anxious, angry, depressed, guilty, upset, bitter, or avoidant *in similar present situations*. We do, however, have the capacity to attack and alter *how* we think about our past.[12] Past events won't become any less real or valid; we can't change the tapes of those events. We can, however, vigorously change how we *think* about them. If you failed or got rejected, or got treated unfairly, admit it and accept it. Then you can move on! (Which *we* will, since much the same argument is true for the tenth screwball belief.)

Irrational Belief No. 10: *"Bad people and things should not exist, but when they do, they have to seriously disturb me!"* That's like saying A's (situations and people) really *do* cause C's (our feelings and behaviors). We already know that, in actuality, the B's (our own thoughts) occur in between, largely determining our C's.

It is admittedly easy to believe that people and things can make you overly angry, anxious, depressed, or guilty—but that belief just doesn't float. Did the boss or your kids, or your spouse or lover or friend, really *make* you overreact? That's not to say that you can't *choose* to get very angry with someone or something. You do, often. But recognizing who is *responsible* for your own feelings (i.e., yourself) enables you to ask: "Is that the way I want to be feeling and acting in this situation?" If the answer is "No!" then what are you going to do to change your irrational *thinking*—a change that will beneficially affect both your feelings *and* your behavior? In the next chapter we'll talk about *how* to do *precisely* that.

[12]With *really* traumatic past experiences, you may need professional help to understand how they are affecting you today, and what you can do to counter them.

EXERCISES

Exercise 4A: Finding the Nutty Beliefs That You Use to Let People and Situations Needlessly Push Your Buttons

As we showed in Chapter 4, we all tend to have at least ten major irrational beliefs that we use to let people needlessly push our buttons. Naturally, you probably don't have *all* of these irrational beliefs, but you'd be surprised how many you *may* believe in specific situations. In this exercise, go over the following list of ten major irrational beliefs, and whenever you find that you have upset yourself and let people needlessly push your buttons, try to see which of these ideas you actually have.

Sample Practice Sheet for Exercise 4A: Finding the Nutty Beliefs That You Use to Let People and Situations Needlessly Push Your Buttons

Irrational Belief	How Often You Believe This		How Strongly You Believe This	
	Seldom	Often	Lightly	Strongly
1) Worrying too much about what other people think of you.				
2) I must not fail at important tasks and if I do it's terrible and I can't stand it.				
3) Low frustration tolerance: people and things should always turn out the way I want them to and if they don't, it's awful, terrible, and horrible and that's not *fair*.				

4) If any of the first three bad events happen then I'll always blame someone for it.

5) If I worry obsessively about some up-coming event or how someone really feels about me things will actually turn out better.

6) Perfect solutions exist for every problem and I must find them and immediately.

7) It is easier to avoid difficult situations and responsibilities than to face them.

8) If I never get seriously involved in anything and maintain a detached perspective, I will never be unhappy.

9) It was my past and all the awful things that happened to me when I was a child or in my last relationship or in my last job that causes me to feel and act this way now.

10) Bad people and things should not exist but when they do, they have to seriously disturb me.

Your Practice Sheet for Exercise 4A: Finding the Nutty Beliefs That You Use to Let People and Situations Needlessly Push Your Buttons

Irrational Belief	How Often You Believe This		How Strongly You Believe This	
	Seldom	Often	Lightly	Strongly
_____	_____		_____	
_____	_____		_____	
_____	_____		_____	
_____	_____		_____	
_____	_____		_____	
_____	_____		_____	
_____	_____		_____	
_____	_____		_____	

Sample Practice Sheet For Exercise 4B: Changing Your Inappropriate to Appropriate Negative Feelings When You Have an Irrational Belief

Examples of Irrational Beliefs	Inappropriate Feelings This Belief Often Produces	Appropriate Feelings You Could Change This To
1) I must always be approved of by people for whom I care.	Worried; rejected.	Concerned; disappointed; sad; determined to "find" other people.
2) I must not fail at important tasks and if I do it's terrible and I can't stand it.	Anxiety; depression.	Concern; regret, frustration.
3) Low Frustration Tolerance: people and things should always turn out the way I want them to and if they don't, it's awful, terrible, and horrible, and that's not *fair*.	Low frustration tolerance; panic; depression; feeling victimized by others.	Frustration; annoyance; irritation; determination to remove frustrations.

Your Practice Sheet for Exercise 4B: Changing Your Inappropriate to Appropriate Negative Feelings When You Have an Irrational Belief

Choose Your Most Frequently Thought Irrational Beliefs	Inappropriate Feelings This Belief Often Produces	Appropriate Feelings You Could Change This To
_____	_____	_____
_____	_____	_____
_____	_____	_____
_____	_____	_____
_____	_____	_____
_____	_____	_____
_____	_____	_____

Sample Practice Sheet for Exercise 4C: Acting Against My Irrational Beliefs

Irrational Belief	Things You Could Do to Act Against This Irrational Belief
1) Worrying too much about what other people think of me.	Take a risk by initiating contact with someone who has been intimidating or difficult, and not make myself anxious about that.
2) I must not fail at important tasks and if I do it's terrible and I can't stand it.	Tell a friend or a colleague about a work failure. Go for an interview for a job I am not sure I'm qualified for. Not upset myself when I've done a job less thoroughly under severe time constraints.
3) Low Frustration Tolerance: people and things should always turn out the way I want them to and if they don't, it's awful, terrible, and horrible, and that's not *fair*.	Stay temporarily in a job or relationship that has real hassles, until I stop upsetting myself about this; and only change the job or relationship when I am clearly not overreacting.

Your Practice Sheet for Exercise 4C: Acting Against My Irrational Beliefs

Choose Your Most Frequently Thought Irrational Beliefs	Things You Could Do to Act Against This Irrational Belief

Chapter 5

How to Change Your Irrational Thinking: Four Steps to Success

Changing your thinking requires commitment, awareness—and practice, practice, practice. Commitment is an attitude that says: (a) "Taking responsibility for my feelings and behavior is essential for me to keep people and things from pushing my buttons." (b) "Learning how to change the way I think in reaction to others is a worthwhile endeavor." (c) "I will stick to it systematically because this is not a one-shot learning experience—it takes time and effort."

Awareness is the first step toward actually changing your thinking. It's unrealistic to expect to change your thinking immediately upon reading about how to do it. Start with situations wherein you already are letting someone or something push your buttons. How are you feeling and acting (Point C)? If you are feeling excessively upset, anxious, angry, depressed, or guilty, do not focus on the person or situation (Point A), but instead ask yourself: "What am I thinking to myself in this situation to get myself upset?" More specifically, ask yourself: "What am I thinking to myself about myself, about the others in the situation, and about the situation?"

Rather than go through these steps for changing thinking abstractly, let's take a real situation from a volunteer in one of our seminars. (As with earlier examples, the statements in brackets are not to be taken as part of the actual thinking the person is doing, but rather as implied—to help you to understand the underlying irrational beliefs supporting the actual thinking in the specific situation.)

Activating Event (A): Joann, a married woman, believed that of late her husband was not being as attentive or loving as usual.

Step 1: At Point C, ask yourself: *How am I inappropriately feeling and acting in this situation?* Joann said she had been making herself extremely anxious, angry, and upset over the past several months. She described herself as being irritable, more withdrawn, uptight, and highly sensitive.

Step 2: At Point B, ask yourself: *What am I thinking to myself to make myself upset?* Joann related her thoughts: "Why is he taking me for granted? What if I'm not as attractive to him as I used to be? That would be awful! Maybe I've let myself go too much. What if he's looking around for someone else? Is it something I've done [that I *should not* have done]? He makes me so mad, acting like that, after I've been as loving as I could be! I always knew he didn't care for me as much as I do for him. What am I going to do? Well, I don't have to stand for this! Who does he think he is? If he doesn't care, then I won't, either!"

It can also be very helpful when identifying your thinking to also figure out which of the first four main irrational beliefs (and any of the other six as well) are underlying and supporting it. For example, Joann realized that fear of rejection, fear of failure, low frustration tolerance, and blame all were contributing to her overreactions. She managed a four-bagger out of this one!

As you can see, when Joann was at home in the actual situation, she jumped around from anxiety to anger to confusion to upsetness. Although her thinking built up over several days, by the time she was done awfulizing, shoulding, and rationalizing about herself, her husband, and the situation, she was ready to kill him the moment he walked in the door!

Now that Joann has identified how she upset herself, she is ready to challenge her thinking by asking as follows:

Step 3: How can I challenge and dispute my irrational thinking?
Joann came up with some great ones: "I do believe that my husband
has not been as attentive or loving lately and seems to be taking me
for granted but is that really awful, terrible, and horrible? Not unless
I make it so. He *may* be less attracted to me than before but even that
is not the end of the world. Although I have no evidence, I cannot
rule out the *possibility* that he could be seeing someone else. Does
getting upset and angry about that *possibility* keep it from being
true? No! If he really doesn't care about me as much, I can talk with
him about that before I assume it's true or feel sorry for myself or
make myself angry. I *can* stand this and I do have other options
besides attacking him or trying to get him back by acting as distant as
he seems to be.

The really *critical* step (and question) follow naturally from Step 3:

*Step 4: What realistic preferences can I substitute for my awfuliz-
ing, shoulding, and rationalizing?* Joann came up with these: " I *want*
my husband to love and respect me very much. If he does, that's
great; but if he doesn't (as much as I'd like), it's not *awful* unless I
make it so. I'd also *like* him to find me attractive—but even if he
again doesn't, that still doesn't mean I'm a reject. I'm very seriously
concerned about what I think is happening between us, and I can talk
with him about it without attacking him or getting *overly* upset. I'd
like him to be more loving, attentive, and appreciative. If he isn't I'm
committed to continuing to try to get what I want in this relationship,
to talking with him about it, to understanding what's going on, and to
resolving this problem. I do not *have to have* his love, I *want* it. If
things don't improve, I would consider leaving—but not until I have
genuinely given it a good try."

Joann is thinking in a *quite* different way with this last set of
thoughts. She has eliminated her awfulizing, shoulding, and rationalizing. She is no longer overreacting. She is, however, still very
seriously concerned with her husband's behavior, and is committed
to dealing with him about it. She has identified what is accurate in
this situation, and has disputed her overreactions. Best of all, she
hasn't tried to con herself into believing it's just all in her imagination, or to deny that anything is going on, or talk herself out of her

legitimate feelings and concerns. The most important difference is that now she can *discuss* the issues with him. With her (original) set of thoughts, she would probably either withdraw and sulk, or start a fight. She was able to change that thinking to realistic preferences, and that made all the difference. She is still very much involved, but now she can deal with that effectively.

It's important to note that in the seminar, Joann did not easily and immediately think through the four steps. She discussed each with a partner, worked hard on each, and concentrated on each. We only reported here the conclusions of her efforts at each step. She actually spent about 20 minutes working through her rethinking. It may take that long when you first start using the steps, but it gets a lot faster as you keep using them. However (as we've said before), this process of changing one's thinking is *not* a "quickie" solution to button-pushing. Joann not only had to concentrate carefully, but (even more importantly) found that she will have to repeat that new set of healthier thoughts over and over again—each time she finds she's starting to upset herself with the original (*and* with new) awfulizing, shoulding, and rationalizing. Actually, it all doesn't take *much* extra time, since you would probably be awfulizing, shoulding, or rationalizing anyway!

One thing we particularly like about Joann's rethinking is that she still can have strong feelings of concern about what is happening with her husband. She also recognizes that she cannot rule out some of her worst concerns, but she is not going to overreact to them. She reaffirms her own feelings for her husband, and commits to dealing with him directly. She even says to herself that if the worst scenarios are true, and he doesn't change, she is prepared to leave the relationship. She does not *want* that option, but she is prepared to exercise it as a last resort—not out of hurt and anger, but because in a good sense, she would not be getting her legitimate wants met.[13]

Figure 1 shows the basic steps you can use to change your thinking in any situation *where someone or something is pushing your*

---

[13]In this particular case, we are assuming that Joann's description of her husband's behavior has been accurate. It is always possible that one's perception of someone else's behavior is distorted or inaccurate, but that can only be clarified by discussion, not fighting.

buttons. It is a condensed outline of what is described in detail immediately afterward.

Step 1: Start at Point C and ask yourself: *"How am I inappropriately feeling and acting in this situation [A] right now?"* Especially look for *excessive* anxiety, anger, depression, guilt, upsetness, hurt, defensiveness, frustration, jealousy, threat, intimidation, withdrawal, procrastination, avoidance, hostility, and the like.

Step 2: Go immediately to Point B and ask yourself: *"What am I irrationally thinking about myself, the others in this situation, or the situation in general, to make myself upset [at point C]?"* Look for your awfulizing, shoulding, or rationalizing especially.

We encourage you to become readily familiar with all ten of the irrational beliefs that we described in Chapter 4—but if that's too many to remember, be sure to know at least the first four, cold: (1) worrying too much about what others think of you (fear of rejection); (2) I must not fail; (3) low frustration tolerance/ "that's not fair"; (4) often blaming someone (yourself or others). These four can help you to figure out what you are thinking that upsets you in a specific situation.

Step 3: Ask yourself: *"How can I challenge and dispute my irrational thinking in Step 1?"* Try asking: "Do I *have* to have.. ?" "*Must* I be...?" "*Should* I...?" "Do I *need* him or her to...?" "*Should* they be...?" "Why is it that I *must* or they *should*...?" "Is it really *awful, terrible,* and *horrible* that I was rejected, or that I failed, or that I didn't get my way, or that I was treated unfairly?" "Why *should* someone be blamed and attacked?" "*Must* I be loved and respected by those I consider important or do I just *want* and *expect* such?" "*Must* I never fail, or do I *want* to succeed?" "*Must* I *never* be treated unfairly, or *would it be better if* I were treated fairly?"

Another way to help you to dispute your overreactions is to accept what *is* accurate in a situation and *not* deny it, avoid it, or exaggerate it. ("My spouse *has* filed for divorce." "I *did* lose my job." "This person *is* being rude and obnoxious." "The kids *are* being pests.") Accepting the valid aspects of a situation can help you to recognize what you are exaggerating, how you are doing that and how you can dispute it: "My spouse *has* filed for divorce, and that's awful and terrible and horrible, and I can't stand it!" But can you *really* not stand it? Do you *have to* have his/her love and affection? Are you *really* a reject? Is the world *always* fair?

Step 4: Ask yourself: *"What realistic preferences can I substitute for my irrational thinking in Step 1?"* Try "I *want*...," "I'd *like*...," "I'd *prefer*...," "It *would be better if*...." You can use feeling words, like: "I regret it...," "It's unfortunate...," I'm disappointed...," I'm seriously concerned...," "I'm committed to...," "It's frustrating [or an inconvenience] that...." By staying with preferences and avoiding awfulizing, terribleizing, horribilizing, shoulding, and rationalizations, you can minimize making yourself excessively anxious, angry, defensive, depressed, and guilty.

These steps may seem lengthy at first, but with just a little practice you will be able to go through all of them in just a few minutes.

Figure 1: Changing Your Nutty Thinking

Step 1: How am I inappropriately feeling and acting in this situation?

Step 2: What am I thinking to make myself upset (overly anxious, angry, depressed, guilty or acting inappropriately):
    (a) about myself?
    (b) about the others?
    (c) about the situation?

Step 3: How can I challenge and dispute my irrational thinking?

Step 4: *What realistic preferences can I substitute for my irrational thinking* (awfulizing, shoulding, and rationalizing)?: "I want...," "I'd like.,." "I'd prefer...," "it would be better if...," What feelings would result?
"It's unfortunate...," "I'm disappointed...," "I'm seriously concerned...," "I regret...," "I'm committed....."

The key to successfully keeping people and things from getting to you is practice, practice, and more practice, in order to change your thinking (and ultimately also your undesired behavior). The nicest payoff for all this effort to redo your thinking is that soon you'll realize that you are not awfulizing, shoulding, and rationalizing *in the first place,* and after a while are much more often starting with realistic preferences automatically.

Now, we don't know of anyone who *never* overreacts, so that category most probably includes you, too. But you can always keep working on *improvement.* Not very many of us are Gandhis. (As a matter of fact, we'll bet that even Gandhi got really ticked off every now and then.) You can become *committed* to getting better and better at not letting people and things push your buttons. Then if you *do* overreact in a situation, even that won't be awful. You can truly regret it, and can *work* on it.

Watch out, though, because *any* system aimed at psychological well-being can be distorted or misapplied. We have seen people come up with "realistic preferences" like "*It would be better if* my ex-spouse got in a train wreck," or "I *want* to die if she doesn't love me anymore."

Sometimes people mistakenly worry that by thinking realistic preferences they will eliminate *all* feelings, and thus become dull, boring, cold, and feelingless. Nothing could be further from the truth! These techniques are designed to eliminate or reduce only your *excessive reactions*—those that get in the way of being able to experience all kinds of wonderful feelings. You sometimes will perceive negative feelings like anger, displeasure, nervousness, frustration, and sadness, too, but not change them into rage, depression, high anxiety, or excessive guilt.

In Steps 1 and 2, you are identifying specifically how you are upsetting yourself and letting people and circumstances push your buttons. Steps 3 and 4 are where you challenge and attack your irrational beliefs and substitute more accurate, rational thoughts and preferences that will keep you from overreacting and making yourself miserable. You can't do this just once and expect miraculous emotional recovery. *Every* time you begin to feel overly upset, and *every* time you act against your own interests, you can go through the four steps and substitute realistic preferences.

Many people ask us: "Is it better to hold it in or let it out?" Our answer every time is *neither!* There is a third option to blowing up, or holding it in and giving yourself an ulcer. Admittedly, it does feel good to let someone have it (especially if they "deserve" it), but that rarely has any lasting benefit, and you become part of the problem. Instead, you can change your emotional overreactions, making them appropriate (self-helping) and effective (enabling you to get more of what you want, and less of what you don't want). Yes, you can actually *change* your feelings, rather than stifle them. Indeed you *are* human—but you do *not* have to make yourself needlessly miserable.

Here now are some examples of how to apply the four-step process in real-life situations. Each example is only one way someone might respond in that situation. As you read through them, see if you can recall similar situations in your life, and apply the four steps to your circumstance as well. Remember: The thoughts in brackets are those *implied* by the actual thinking.

Divorce: A Potential Four-Bagger

You are going through a divorce. It has been a difficult and painful experience, but *seems* like the right choice. Nevertheless, you often are upset.

Step 2: How am I feeling and acting?

Appropriately: Sorry, disappointed, sad.

Inappropriately: Overly angry, anxious, depressed, and guilty [a four-bagger!]. "I am on edge, easily distracted, less productive, withdrawn, and sometimes short-tempered."

Step 2: What irrational beliefs am I thinking to get myself overly anxious, angry, depressed, guilty, and less productive?

a: "What am I irrationally thinking about myself?"

"Oh, my God, what have I done? *I've ended 14 years of my life. I should* have been a better spouse, and not wrecked this marriage! This is terrible! What if I made a mistake? What if I wind up alone for the rest of my life? That would be *awful!* What if I can't even support myself? How am I going to take care of this whole house? What a mess I've made of this! This is just *horrible!* I *can't stand* being so lonely. I feel so empty. I'm a failure. Nothing matters anymore; I've ruined everything!"

b: What am I irrationally thinking about the others?

"What if little Billy is permanently affected by this? What if I can't be both parents for him? What if he hates me for this? I couldn't take that! I *should* have thought more about him than myself."

About ex-husband: "That creep—I hate him! He probably never really cared. He didn't even care enough to try to make it work. I hate him! I hate him! How could he do this to me? I hope he's miserable!"

About friends/relatives: "They probably all think I'm a failure. I'll never see them again. I can't face them. They won't want anything to do with me [and they're right!]."

c: What am I thinking about the situation?

"It's not fair: I gave this relationship the best years of my life! What do I do now? Have I dug my own grave? I dread going to court and dragging out the gory details. And when John comes over to pick up Billy, I just get terribly upset. I can't bear the whole rotten mess!"

Step 3: How can I challenge and dispute my irrational beliefs?

"I *am* getting divorced and my life is greatly changed, but do I really *have* to have someone in my life? No! Being unmarried, am I only part of a person? No! Have I permanently impaired my son? Very unlikely! Am *I* a failure? No, even though in some respects I may have failed. *Should* my husband be severely punished? *No!* Am I forever incapable of handling my finances and house maintenance? No! *Should* I have hung in there? Most probably not! Does nothing matter, really?"

Step 4: What realistic preferences can I substitute for my irrational thinking?

"I'd *like* to have someone to love, but I don't *have to* in order to be happy. I don't *want* to be alone or lonely, but if I *am* alone, I *can* handle it. It's *not* awful, terrible, or horrible unless I make it so."

"I'd *like* my son to come through this unfortunate event, and I will do everything I can to make that happen—but awfulizing about it will not make it any better. He'll survive!"

"I'd *prefer* to have worked it out, but we didn't. I am seriously concerned about my future, but I am not going to make myself miserable about it. I deeply regret that this is happening, but I am committed to getting on with my life."

If you continue to substitute realistic preferences every time you start awfulizing, shoulding, or rationalizing, you will be able to handle *all* kinds of difficult situations: explaining things to your child, dealing with your ex-spouse, being with either well-intentioned *or* disapproving relatives and friends, and taking on functions and responsibilities that can help you to get on with your life. You would rarely have blowups, depressions, anxiety attacks, or pangs of guilt. You might of course feel frustrated, displeased, sad, concerned, and committed to both your present and your future happiness. But in each challenging situation you would reiterate both your realistic preferences and your commitment to handling not only that moment but the future, too.

Now, *you* might not think all the thoughts that we presented in Step 2 if *you* were going through a divorce, but then you might at least think *some* of them—and even they most assuredly would push your buttons if you did! The thoughts presented here are a compilation of real-life examples from people as they *did* go through divorce. You might instead have had a similar ending to a serious relationship. What pushed your buttons at times: what were *your* thoughts? The focus here is to see how you can *use* the four-step process for Changing Your Thinking. Here's another situation.

"What Have You Done for Me Lately?"

Your 13-year-old son comes home from school. The first seven sentences out of his mouth are: (1) "What's for dinner?" (2) "I need a ride to Jimmy's—I left my bike over there the other day." (3) "I've got to get some of those new pump-up tennis shoes all the guys are wearing; they're only $170." (4) Joey wants to spend the night—OK?" (5) "I need some money to go play video games with the guys." (6) "How come all my jeans are still in with the dirty clothes?" (7) "A bunch of the guys are going to the basketball game Saturday night and I told them you'd give us a ride." No "Hi, Mom!" or "Thanks!" or (perish the thought), "How are you?"

Step 1: How am I feeling and acting?

Appropriately: Frustrated, and annoyed at his behavior.

Inappropriately: Irate and victimized. Snap at him, withdraw to the bathroom and scream, do a slow burn until I finally blow up, or get on his case for something else (his room, his homework, his chores, his friends).

Step 2: What am I irrationally thinking to myself to get myself excessively anxious, angry, depressed, or guilty?

a: What am I irrationally thinking to myself?

"I'm just a slave around here. I'm sick and tired of 'do this, do that for me!' I'm not Cinderella! I won't be treated like dirt anymore! I've had it." Or perhaps: "What a rotten mother I must be to have a son like him. I didn't do anything right."

b: What am I irrationally thinking about the others?

"Who does he think he is? He walks in and starts demanding everything! 'Do *this.* I need *that.*' He's just a spoiled brat. 'Gimme, gimme, gimme!' And if I say no, he tries to make me feel guilty. [What a louse he is!] He's driving me crazy. I hate it when he's so selfish. It's as if we *owe* it to him!"

c: What am I irrationally thinking about the situation?

This whole thing is crazy. The tail's wagging the dog. All I do is take care of *his* needs. I hardly have a life of my own."

Step 3: How can I challenge and dispute my irrational beliefs?

"He *is* very self-centered and demanding, and rarely shows appreciation, but does that mean I *have to* blow up or feel victimized? No! Will either help? No! Will picking on him for other things, *or* ignoring them, make him change? No!"

Step 4: What realistic preferences can I substitute for my irrational thinking?

"I *want* him to appreciate my efforts more. I'd *like* him to balance his giving and taking better, but I don't have to overreact if he doesn't. I know he has to depend on me for lots of things, but I also want him to appreciate what I do to help him. I'd *like* him to be more sensitive to others in general—but it's not awful, terrible, and horrible that he isn't—it's only frustrating. I am *committed* to getting him to be more thoughtful and appreciative, but if I don't succeed, I don't have to blow up and become part of the problem."

This situation is such a typical one that it's almost just part of normal parenting. It often comes with the turf. It is true that kids tend to be self-absorbed, *but* we can do a great deal to minimize this occurrence and to prevent its getting to us. By thinking in terms of preferences we can still confront our children's behavior, discuss our concerns, clarify our expectations, and punish extreme inconsiderate behavior if it persists.

The most important thing is that you can do all this without overreacting or losing your cool! You might wind up saying to your child, "David, when you fire off six or seven things you want, without even a hello or thanks, it looks to me like you're taking me for granted—and I don't like that." Depending on how your child (let's say you have a boy named David) responds, you might then say, "I can understand that you need us for a lot of these things, but I'd like you to appreciate that fact, and show it more often."

If your son is sarcastic or defensive, you might choose to confront him with "David, your indifferent [or sarcastic] attitude about what I said is just what I'm talking about. I'm not willing to do [fill in the words] for you as long as you don't appreciate it." Don't say it as if you're childishly getting back at him or playing games. Say it directly, honestly, calmly, and firmly. Then be sure you do as you promise: Consistency between what you *say* and what you *do* is critical!

Here's an interesting point. Take this same situation and, instead of awfulizing and shoulding about it in Step 2, try some rationalizations: "He *is* only 13, and he *does* have to depend on me a lot. I was probably the same way myself when I was his age. I guess this is just part of being the parent of a teenager. At least I can be thankful that he's not into drugs or alcohol, or worse. Only five more years before he's on his own [I hope]."

The underlying screwball belief for these rationalizations would be: "It's easier to avoid difficult situations like confronting him, because he might not like me, or get upset with me." Step 3's "disputing" would then be: "Is it really better in the long run to avoid dealing with him? No! Is he really responsible for his behavior? He is!" Consequently, your substitute realistic preferences would also include: "It's *not* easier to avoid this situation—and, even though it's uncomfortable, it's important to confront him. He *is* responsible for how he acts toward me, and I *want* to show him that."

In either case (whether awfulizing and shoulding or rationalizing), by challenging and disputing your own thinking, and substituting realistic preferences, you are much more likely to confront his behavior and in an effective manner.

Now let's take a look at a situation that often happens on the job. So often it's not the work itself that gets to us, it's the *people* with whom we work that we allow to push our buttons.

Clash of the Psyches (Not the Psychos)

You have a personality clash with a person who works with you. You're not quite sure why, but it seems that you just can't get along—you just don't like each other. This situation is affecting your work, in that he is less and less cooperative and helpful, and you both seem to argue over insignificant issues. Communication and productivity are suffering.

Step 1: How are you feeling and acting?

Appropriately: Sorry and frustrated.

Inappropriately: Overly angry, upset, argumentative, withdrawn, sarcastic, and defensive.

Step 2: What am I irrationally thinking to make myself overly anxious, angry, depressed, guilty, withdrawn, sarcastic, and defensive?

a: What am I irrationally thinking about myself?

"I'm an idiot! I *shouldn't* let this jerk get to me. I *shouldn't* be so immature. Why *should* I care about it at all?"
And/or: "I'm not going to take this stuff from him or anybody! I can't let him get the upper hand! I'll show him!"

b: What am I thinking about the others in the situation?

"I just *can't stand* this creep. He makes me so mad I could kill him. How he got his job is beyond me. He must have something on someone higher up. What if he keeps up this conflict and it gets worse? He just doesn't give a darn about anything or anybody but himself [and he *shouldn't* be that way! That bastard!]."

c: What am I irrationally thinking about the situation?

"This job used to be fun. What if *I* get in trouble because *my* work isn't up to par because of *his* lack of cooperation? I can't win for trying. I don't deserve this. The more I try to get along, the worse it gets. If I ignore him, he gets more difficult and he wins the battle. Yuk!"

Step 3: How can I challenge and dispute my irrational thinking?

"There's no question that we are not getting along, but can I really not stand it? Am I contributing to the conflict by getting myself upset? *Must* he act the way I think he *should* act, and is it really *awful*, or am I making it awful if he doesn't?"

Step 4: What realistic preferences can I substitute for my irrational thinking?

"I *want* him to be more cooperative, and I'd *like* us to get along better. If we do, great! If we don't, its not awful, terrible, and horrible. It's unfortunate, and I regret it. I'm concerned about this situation, and I am *committed* to improving the relationship.

"If nothing gets better, I don't *have to* to make myself miserable as well! I don't *have to* 'should' on him, nor do I have to awfulize. *It would be better* if my work was unaffected by this conflict, and I will do everything I can to prevent that—but if it *is* affected, I can handle that. I will continue to communicate directly, honestly, and respectfully with him. I don't have to *like* him to do that. I would like to be treated as well as I treat him, but if I'm not, it's unfortunate but not horrible. I will talk with him about what's going on, and try hard to resolve it. If we do, great! If we don't—I'll live!" (If necessary, you might get a third party involved, as a mediator—not to prove who is right, but to help resolve the conflict.)

The preceding situation is incredibly common. Notice that there are two main courses of action: (1) Do everything possible to communicate better, get along, and not be part of the problem yourself. (2) Change your thinking so that you don't let your co-worker push your buttons if *he* doesn't change. Usually you won't accomplish the first without successfully doing the second. Changing your thinking is between you and *you*. It has little to do with your coworker.

Now, nobody's perfect at this kind of self-control. Remember, the goal is to reduce your overreactions. You may still feel appropriately frustrated and irritated—and these feelings are admittedly negative, but they also are reasonable, and may even motivate you to keep working to improve the situation. But you will not be letting your coworker push your buttons and thereby "make you" miserable. Especially remember that you can still confront him when he acts badly and you are still going to do all you can to get this situation corrected. Just refuse to let him bug you! And you don't do that by either ignoring him or making a New Year's resolution, but by *changing your thinking.*

Now comes a situation that might get to you in a *very* personal way.

The Critic

You have a good friend (or lover) who is an interesting, really alive, stimulating person. You enjoy her company, and she has many fine qualities—but she often is critical, negative, or sarcastic toward you. She frequently implies that you are not intelligent or you're wrong, or you've got poor judgment, or you didn't handle something right.

You get together at your place, which you've just spent thousands of dollars to redecorate. She spends much of the time making digs and expressing disbelief in your taste and judgment. She's not flagrantly attacking, but you clearly get the message that she often disapproves not only of what you do, but also of you for doing it.

Step 1: How am I feeling and acting if I let her push my buttons?

Appropriately: Displeased and frustrated about what she's doing.

Inappropriately: Overly angry at her, hurt, defensive, and fed up.

Step 2: What am I irrationally thinking to make myself excessively anxious, angry, depressed, guilty, defensive or vindictive?

a: What am I irrationally thinking about myself?

"What if I am as stupid as she thinks? Maybe she's right and I'm just being defensive."

b: What am I irrationally thinking about the others?

"No, it's not me, it's she! She shouldn't be that critical! I just hate her when she's so negative! She drives me crazy with that sarcastic tone. She's just a phony! She has to put everyone down because she's so insecure herself!"

c: What am I irrationally thinking about the situation?

"With friends like this, who needs enemies? I *shouldn't* have to stand for this garbage! Being friends with her isn't worth it. This is it! I've had it! This is the last time I let her put me down! She's *got* to stop it; she's driving me nuts!" (The underlying beliefs here are "It's not fair as it should be!" and fear of rejection and failure.)

Step 3: How can I challenge and dispute my irrational thinking?

"Although she *is* often negative and sarcastic, is it really *awful* that she is? No. Do I *have to* please her or have her approval? No! Do I *have to* let her push my buttons, or can *I* decide how I'll react? Can she actually drive me crazy, or do *I* make myself miserable when she is so critical?"

Step 4: What realistic preferences can I substitute for my irrational thinking?

"I'd *like* her to be more positive, and to drop her sarcasm and criticism. I do *want* honest opinions, but not putdowns. It's frustrating that she's negative so frequently. I *want* her to stop it, but I can certainly stand it. I can confront her about this without blowing up. If she changes, then we can continue our friendship, but if she doesn't, I may well end it. That would be sad, but not awful. I am really committed to trying to improve this friendship before I give up [low frustration tolerance] and end it too quickly."

When someone like this pushes your buttons, you may often either rationalize it because you are afraid to confront this person, or you "gunnysack" it until one time you finally let her have it for all the times she was sarcastic. Thinking realistic preferences enables you to confront her in a functional and serious manner without overreacting. You are then assertive but not hostile and aggressive. Then, you will increase the chances of getting the person to change *and* you can feel really good about the way *you* handled it.

You might say to her, "Listen—I know you have strong convictions about lots of things, but when you criticize me in a sarcastic and sometimes condescending manner, I find myself reacting more to the demeaning way you are saying it than to what it is you are saying."

As in any similar situation, what you choose to say next depends on how she responds to you now. If she takes it well, or is only mildly defensive, you might say, "I *am* interested in your candid opinions, but I'd like to discuss them with you without your being sarcastic or condescending. Will you do that?" If she is still sarcastic or condescending in her response, then say perhaps, "The way you just responded is an example of what I'm talking about, and I'd really like you to talk to me differently, but still express your honest opinions. Will you do *that?*" In both cases you will have been direct and somewhat confrontive, but at lease you did not overreact—nor did you lose control of the situation. If she persists, you may decide that the friendship isn't worth the hassle, and end it. But you will have done so thoughtfully, not fitfully.

Now that you know the principles and skills needed to keep people and things from pushing your buttons, it's time to *apply* them. In the following chapters we'll show how to apply the basic skills in some of the typical situations we all face. This is where we get down to what counts: using these skills in our real, day-to-day lives.

EXERCISES

Exercise 5A: Identifying Your Inappropriate Feelings and Behaviors and Discovering Your Irrational Thinking: The First Two Steps to Success

This exercise will give you practice identifying your inappropriate feelings and Behaviors and then discovering (which is followed by challenging/disputing and changing) your irrational thinking. Think of specific pertinent situations in which you tend to overreact emotionally and/or behaviorally, and then identify what you are irrationally thinking at that time.

Sample Practice Sheet for Exercise 5A: Identifying Your Inappropriate Feelings and Behaviors and Discovering Your Irrational Thinking: The First Two Steps to Success

Unfortunate Situation	Identify Your Inappropriate Feelings and Behaviors	State Your Irrational Thinking at That Time
Being rejected by someone I care for.	Self-downing; anger; depression.	I'm devastated. How can I go on without him/her? Will anybody ever *really* love me? I'm a real loser.
Being criticized at work.	Panic; depression; urge to quit job.	I must not be criticized! They think I'm incompetent and they are right! I'll never do any job well.
Not being able to buy a car I really want	Anger; depression.	I *must* have that car and no other! It's not fair! I've got to have it.

Your Practice Sheet for Exercise 5A: Identifying Your Inappropriate Feelings and Behaviors and Discovering Your Irrational Thinking: The First Two Steps to Success

Unfortunate Situation	Identify Your Inappropriate Feelings and Actions	State Your Irrational Thinking at That Time

Sample Practice Sheet for Exercise 5B: Challenging and Disputing Your Irrational Thinking: Step 3 to Success

Irrational Belief	Challenging and Disputing Your Irrational Belief
When people criticize me, that makes me an incompetent person.	It may make me a person who's *acting* *in*competently right now, but even if that is true, how does that make me a *totally incompetent* person? Do I have to do everything right? If I don't, do I have to get upset when it is pointed out that I failed?
I can't stand to be criticized at work.	Why *must* I not be? Even if people wrongly criticize me, can I really not stand it? I can't control other people, but I can control myself.
I must have that particular car and no other car.	Why *must* I? It would be lovely if I could have just the car I want, but why must the universe provide it for me?

Your Practice Sheet for Exercise 5B: Challenging and Disputing Your
Irrational Thinking: Step 3 to Success

| | Challenging and Disputing |
Irrational Belief	Your Irrational Belief
_____	_____
_____	_____
_____	_____
_____	_____
_____	_____
_____	_____
_____	_____
_____	_____
_____	_____

Sample Practice Sheet for Exercise 5C: Changing Your Irrational Thinking: Step 4 to Success

Irrational Belief	Realistic Preferences I Can Substitute for Your Irrational Beliefs
When someone I'm interested in rejects me, I can't bear it!	I *prefer* people to approve of or love me, but I don't *need* that approval. I *can* bear disapproval and be less happy but still find much happiness in life and also find others who *will* like me.
I must not be criticized at work.	I would like to be appreciated at work but I don't *have* to be. I'll try to use this criticism to improve my performance. Even if I don't improve and they still criticize me, I am determined to accept valid criticisms and not be defensive.
I must have that particular car and no other car.	I'd greatly prefer that particular car but can also enjoy another car. My life hardly depends on having that one!

Your Practice Sheet for Exercise 5C: Changing Your Irrational Thinking: Step 4 to Success

Irrational Belief	Realistic Preferences You Can Substitute for Your Irrational Beliefs

Chapter 6

How to Keep People and Things From Pushing Your Buttons on the Job

The world of work is so very different for each of us, yet we all have people and things that push our buttons there. Sometimes it's just the *way* we're treated by a boss, a colleague, or a supervisor. Sometimes it's a boss who is always playing CYA ("Cover Your Flanks"—that's close enough), or doesn't listen to anyone's ideas, or is the least competent person in the department, or is a pompous dictator, or is extremely indecisive. Maybe it's a supervisor or a colleague who is indifferent about his or her work and keeps you from getting yours done, or maybe it's a coworker whose performance is acceptable but who is a royal pain to work with.

When you think about "human" button-pushers, you can start with the generic term "difficult people" and then think of the more specific types that bug you—like know-it-alls; whiners; complainers; nonsupporters; manipulators; irresponsible/lazy/indifferent, incompetent, overly critical/negative, condescending/pompous, gossipy, insensitive, overly sensitive, uncooperative/stubborn, and intimidating people; victims; creeps; and slugs. This is just a sampling of the many kinds of people we can let drive us crazy at work. Hopefully, we don't have one of each!

At other times, it's some "thing" that gets to us—like unreasonable expectations from bosses, boring meetings, multiple or changing priorities, heavy workloads, frequent deadlines, future uncertainties, office politics, constant interruptions, and/or heavy responsibility with little authority. We spend more and more of our time at work (more than 46 hours a week on average, according to recent studies) and although we may not care as deeply for our colleagues as we do for our loved ones, we still want their *respect*, and can surely use their *help*. Because of that, they have great potential to push our buttons. In every occupation, from entry-level jobs (secretaries, clerks, production-line workers, unskilled technicians) to top-level executive positions, and everything in between, people can push our buttons daily. But only if we *let* them!

Here are several situations that workers have often cited in our Rational Effectiveness Training seminars. You can see how these people worked through the four-step process to get control of their overreactions.

The Empty Suit

You work closely with five other people in your department, but you don't hire, evaluate, or fire them. You have one person, Jim, who constantly makes the same mistakes. He also takes much longer than expected to get tasks done but seems indifferent to it all. He in fact affects both your efficiency and the productivity of the whole office. In the corporate world these people are called "empty suits."

Step 1: How am I feeling and acting?

Appropriately: Frustrated and annoyed at Jim's behavior, and checking with others to see if you are observing it correctly.

Inappropriately: Enraged at Jim, helpless, disgusted, bad-mouthing Jim, making sarcastic comments, isolating him (giving him the cold shoulder), and not including him in discussions about work. Down about Jim's causing you and the others to be less productive, and about your boss's blaming *you* for this.

Step 2: What am I thinking to make myself overly anxious, angry, depressed, guilty, and uncooperative?

   a: What am I thinking about myself?

   "I really hate it when Jim keeps screwing up day after day with the same stupid mistakes. But what else can I do? I've tried as hard as I can to help him. What if *I* start getting poor evaluations because *he's* making us all look bad? [That would be *awful*. He *shouldn't* make the rest of us look bad!]"

   b: What am I irrationally thinking about Jim and my coworkers?

   "This guy is hopeless. He's a lost cause, and he doesn't even care [and he *ought to*]. He *should* quit if he had a brain. The boss *has got to* see how bad Jim is and *should* have the guts to get rid of him, but he doesn't even know how bad Jim really is. What a dunce!"

   c: What am I irrationally thinking about the situation?

   "I keep getting caught in the middle between an incompetent and a boss who won't do anything. That really stinks! It's just not fair! Why should I suffer because Jim and the boss don't do their jobs but only prolong this stupid situation?"

Step 3: How can I challenge and dispute my irrational thoughts?

   "Jim makes the same mistakes over and over, but doesn't seem to care—plus, the boss has avoided dealing with him. But does making myself irate help me to handle it better, or get him to shape up? Does demeaning him to others improve the situation? Is sitting around complaining about the boss a real solution? *Must* they be the way I expect them to be—but if they aren't, *must* I be miserable?"

Step 4: What realistic preferences can I substitute for my irrational thinking?

   "I'd *like* Jim to be more competent, and to care about the quality of his work. I am *seriously concerned* about Jim's effect on *my* ability to get *my* work done, and I'd better figure out how I can say something to him to get him to change. If that doesn't work, I will tactfully talk to my boss—without overreacting and without accusing him of being a rotten boss—for not handling Jim better."

If you were awfulizing and shoulding, you would likely get yourself really disgusted, and finally let Jim have it with both barrels. Or you might well go to the boss and dump on *him.* Or you might devise some sneaky way to make life miserable for Jim, so that he leaves—or else find a way to stick some other department with him.

If you were rationalizing, you might too easily keep giving Jim the benefit of the doubt, and just tolerate the situation, doing nothing about it.

If you were thinking in terms of realistic preferences, however, you might either confront Jim directly, or talk with the boss. In confronting Jim, you might say: "When you keep making the same mistakes [specify what they are] and you don't change, I'm not able to get my part of our work done efficiently, and I'm seriously concerned about that."

If Jim is defensive or indifferent, you can say, "I understand that we all make mistakes. But now, there are so many of them that none of us is able to do our job well."

If Jim acts offended that you—a mere equal—are hassling him, say, "You're right; I'm not your boss. But what's happening *is* affecting your, my, and everyone else's job; and I want to work with you to improve things."

If you get a "Drop dead!" from Jim, you might say, "I'd rather work this out between us—but if you refuse to even discuss it, I'm willing to bring the boss in on this. I'd much rather resolve it between us, but if you reject that, I'm not going to ignore the problem. Let's try to deal with it between us."

Although this may sound like a threat, you are really saying that you want to solve it here and now, with no others involved, but that if Jim refuses, you won't roll over and blow away. This is a touchy conflict situation, and you can see how important it is to not let him push your buttons—and also for you not to angrily put him down, as you confront him. You *can* talk to him assertively, and do it with respect!

The following are some other situations that often push people's buttons on the job. After reading these, identify one or two real-life work situations that have gotten to you, and proceed through the four steps on your own. Then go get 'em!

Getting Punished for Doing Good Work

You are a very efficient and productive worker. Your boss (in this instance a woman) keeps giving you more and more work to do, to the point where you are really overloaded. Moreover, you see others in the office who aren't nearly as overworked. The boss even admits to giving you the work precisely because you are so good at handling so much.

Step 1: How am I feeling and acting?

Appropriately: Frustrated, taken advantage of, pressured.

Inappropriately: Overly angry and resentful. Irritable with others, short with the boss, testy at home, sarcastic with under-worked colleagues and critical of them to others. Panicked about possibly not doing well enough to keep the boss happy.

Step 2: What am I irrationally thinking to make myself overly anxious, angry, depressed, guilty, and sarcastic?

a: What am I irrationally thinking about myself?

"Why should I be punished with more work, just because I do a good job? When I get home, I'm exhausted. I'm not a machine, and I *shouldn't* be treated like this! I can't take much more. This job is making me a nervous wreck!"

b: What am I irrationally thinking about the others?

"My boss *should* give more work to the others, and get rid of them if they can't do it right. She's *got to* lighten up on me. What if I complain and she fires me? That would be awful! She probably doesn't even care, as long as it all gets done."

c: What am I irrationally thinking about the situation?

"It's just not fair [and it *should* be]. I can't win, no matter what I do. Something's *got to* change!"

Step 3: How can I challenge and dispute my irrational thinking?

"Although it's *not* fair that I am given more work than the others, do I *need to* greatly upset myself as well? *Must* my boss be fair in the distribution of work, or do I very much *want* her to be fair? And if she isn't fair, *must* I become a nervous wreck? Where is it written that if I'm treated unfairly, I need to make myself miserable?"

Step 4: What realistic preferences can I substitute for my irrational, self-defeating thoughts?

"It *would be a lot better* if the boss distributed the work more evenly. I'd *like* her not to overload me just because I do good work. She obviously doesn't *have to* balance the work loads, but I very much *want* her to. I am committed to discussing my concerns with her without blaming her or shoulding on her, and without sounding like I'm whining. If she understands and agrees to balance the work better, super. If she is defensive or indifferent, then I will decide whether I am willing to stay on under these conditions."

This situation is so very common, and is an especially good one to cite because someone else could just as easily rationalize in the exact same circumstances. Here's one way it could go:

Step 1: How am I feeling and acting?

Appropriately: Frustrated.

Inappropriately: Avoidant, inactive, procrastinating.

Step 2: What am I irrationally thinking to make myself indifferent, inactive, and procrastinate?

a: What am I irrationally thinking about myself?

"I really shouldn't complain; that would look bad. Maybe I'm just not trying hard enough. I should be more efficient—then it wouldn't be so much work. If I do really well here, I may get a raise or even a promotion. I should be happy that my boss thinks that highly of me. If I did say something he might be offended, and I'd be ruined here."

b: What am I irrationally thinking about the others?

"My boss is probably too busy to even notice my problems. She's got enough to worry about without my rocking the boat. The others know I'm up to my eyeballs in work. Maybe someone will offer to help."

c: What are you irrationally thinking about the situation?

"Maybe it's just temporary. I guess we all have to pay our dues in the trenches. Maybe it will get better soon. Somebody has to do it."

Step 3: How can I challenge and dispute my irrational thinking?

"Why *shouldn't* I assert myself, even though it *might* not be well received? Could it be worse for me if I don't speak up? Is my boss really too busy, or am I avoiding an uncomfortable situation? Is it really *too hard* to face this? No, it's only difficult and I *can* do it. Will the situation likely change if I do nothing about it? Fat chance!"

Step 4: What realistic preferences can I substitute for my irrational thoughts?

"I would *like* the boss to correct these imbalances herself, and I'd *like* others to volunteer to help when they can. I am *seriously concerned* about the amount of work I am given, because it is interfering with the quality of my performance. I will discuss the issue with my boss, without blowing up or whining. It is easy to avoid difficult situations, but not in the long run. I can handle whatever the boss says in response when I bring it up."

Awfulizing and shoulding in this situation could lead to sarcastically complaining to your colleagues or your boss, or even quitting in a huff. Rationalizations might lead you to say nothing and keep taking it until you get into more difficulties, or quit impulsively. Thinking realistic preferences enables you to discuss the problem with your boss without whining or griping or sounding like *you* are the problem.

Once you give up thinking irrationally and feeling disturbed, you could say to your boss, "When you give me more work than the others, and more than I can handle, I find myself not doing as thorough a job, and being heavily pressured to meet the deadlines— and I am seriously concerned about this. I'm also frustrated that others are not nearly as busy. I understand and appreciate your confidence in my being able to get things done, but I would really like to see a better balance in the distribution of work."

You might also ask your coworkers in a direct, honest, and respectful (not accusatory or sarcastic) manner to help you. If you get no cooperation from either source, the ball is in your court. Whatever you choose to do, you can refuse to make yourself miserable even if you continue to be treated unfairly by your boss.

This Is the Big One!

You are nervously waiting in the outer office to go into a very important job interview. Getting the position will lead to a much higher salary, a great opportunity for advancement, and challenging, interesting work. You know that there are two other finalists. This is the chance of a lifetime!

Step 1: How am I feeling and acting?

Appropriately: Concerned, and determined to do your best in the first interview.

Inappropriately: Extremely anxious. My foot is twitching a mile a minute. I am sweating profusely.

Step 2: What am I irrationally thinking to make myself overly anxious, angry, depressed, or guilty?

a: What am I irrationally thinking about myself?

"What if I blow it? What if I say something that offends the interviewer without my even knowing it? What if I don't get a chance to show my strong points? What if I don't get the job? What if I *do* get the job?

"I *have to* get this job! It will be *horrible* if I don't! I have to do something to beat out those two other finalists! Look at me—I'm shaking like a leaf. I just know I'm going to blow it. I must not show how nervous I am! Mother was right: I'll never amount to anything!"

b: What am I irrationally thinking about the others?

"What if the interviewer makes a snap judgment? What if he has already decided? What if he asks me trick questions? What if he is really strange? What if he is prejudiced against me? That would be awful!"

c: What am I irrationally thinking about the situation?

"I just hate interviews. They're so fake. You can't really get to know anyone that fast. They shouldn't even be part of getting a job! It's all so ridiculous. I don't even care if I get the stupid job!"

Step 3: How can I challenge and dispute my irrational thoughts?

"This is a really great opportunity, but is it devastating if I don't get it? Does catastrophizing about it help get me the job? Is it absolutely essential that I not be nervous at all in the interview? Even though interviews can be limited and superficial, is there any reason why they shouldn't exist? Can I manage to do my best and have a good interview?"

Step 4: What realistic preferences can I substitute for my irrational thinking?

"I would *like* to do well in the interview. I would very much *like* to get the job. If I do, wonderful; if I don't, I will be really disappointed, but not horrified. I would like to learn something from this interview experience—but even if I don't learn a thing, it's still not the end of the world, and I don't have to upset myself unless I indulge in awfulizing and shoulding. I'm not crazy about interviews, but I *can* live with them without overreacting."

If you do awfulize and should in the outer office, you will likely be fidgeting or riffling through a (probably upside-down) magazine. In the interview itself, maybe you will spill the coffee they give you, or go to shake hands with the interviewer and poke him in the stomach, or go totally blank when he asks a fairly simple question. Immediately after the interview is over, you will remember 20 other things you *should* have pointed out. If you rationalize beforehand really hard ("so what, who cares, big deal"), you might come across as aloof or indifferent—as though you really don't care, when all you were trying to do was cover up your anxiety by seeming to be "cool."

By thinking realistic preferences you may still be somewhat anxious, but you will be able to get your anxiety down to a level where you are clear-headed and can respond to questions in an articulate and enthusiastic manner. Interviewers will react to how you "come across," as well as what you are saying. It makes much more sense to actually reduce your anxiety inside than to try to fake it outside. Thinking realistic preferences works great to get that anxiety down to an unpanicked, manageable level.

The Whiners

Two people in your work group constantly complain and whine about everything. They seem to feed off of each other, and they try to draw you and others into their negativity. They talk about everybody else to you, and you know they do the same about you to others. They waste enormous amounts of time, often distracting the group from its work, getting everyone else upset, and creating a very negative work atmosphere. One of them comes to you for the fourth time today (while you are trying to get your own work done), moaning, "Wait until you hear what they're making us do now!" You have finally had it!

Step 1: How am I feeling and acting?

Fed up, angry, disgusted. About to tell them what I really think of them in no uncertain terms, and storm off.

Step 2: What am I thinking to make myself excessively anxious, angry, depressed, guilty, and hostile?

a: What am I thinking about myself?

"I cannot take this anymore! I can't listen to this bull one more minute! I'm just trying to do my job while these jerks are sitting around griping to everybody and driving me absolutely crazy!"

b: What am I thinking about the others?

"Whine, complain, moan, gripe. That's all they ever do. They shouldn't be allowed to get away with any of that crap! How can they be such dorks?"

c: What am I thinking about the situation?

"This has become a horrible place to work in! I hate it! I don't even look forward to coming to work anymore! This whining and griping *ought to* be outlawed. It's got to stop!"

Step 3: How can I challenge and dispute my irrational thoughts?

"These two do whine and complain a lot, but are they really driving me crazy, or am I driving me crazy when they do it? Even though I greatly dislike it, can I really not stand it? Does getting upset with them stop it in the long run, or is there a better way?"

Step 4: What realistic preferences can I substitute for my irrational thinking?

"I'd like them not to whine and complain so much, and not to set such a negative tone around here. I want them to realize the effect they have on the group, and I really want them to know how annoying it is to listen to their whining. But if they persist, I can largely ignore them, can let the boss know what is going on, can confront them—or, if nothing else works, look for a job with better conditions."

This is a great example because the whiners' behavior is something to be legitimately frustrated and displeased about. But if you keep awfulizing and shoulding about it, you will likely blow up and make things worse. The whiners will then have gotten to you, you will be as negative as they are, and you will give them something to *really* whine about to others. However, if you think in terms of realistic preferences, you can still confront them, but without attacking them. You simply say something like: "When you continually complain about the things that are happening here, I find myself enjoying talking with you less and less, and that's frustrating to me. I'd like to talk with you, but I'd like you to discuss and not complain. I'd like to solve problems, not just be negative. Will you do that with me?"

Frankly, you may get all kinds of defensiveness, excuses, more whining, or even hurt responses. Or you also might get a cooperative response. Whatever you get, *you* handled the situation well, and you did not let them push your buttons. On the other hand, enraging yourself with the brief pleasure of letting someone have it who desperately "deserves" it is not as valuable (or pleasurable) as the ability to truly keep your cool. In the above illustration, you were able to express your valid criticism without being abusive. Now, that's really worth something!

Check Chapter 2's Exercises section for some more situations you can let push your buttons, and several different ways you *could* respond (depending on how you *think* about them).

EXERCISES

Exercise: Changing Your Emotional and Behavioral Overreactions and Your Irrational Thinking About Your Job, Business, or Profession

These exercises will give you practice in discovering and changing your feelings, actions, and irrational thinking about your job, business, or profession. First, think of specific pertinent situations in which you tend to overreact, then identify what you are irrationally thinking at that time.

Sample Practice Sheet for Exercise 6A: Discovering Your Emotional and Behavioral Overreactions and Your Irrational Thinking About Your Job, Business, or Profession

Specific Situation	Your Emotional and Behavioral Overreactions	Your Irrational Thinking at That Time
Being criticized by my boss or supervisor for something I did badly.	Shame; anxiety; depression; absence from work; avoidance of my boss.	I'm just no good at this and I'll never be able to do better. I have to improve or else I'm unemployable. This is really awful.
Being unjustly criticized by my boss or supervisor when I didn't do badly.	Extreme anger; talking nastily about your boss or supervisor. (Later, feel guilty about overreaction.	That lousy supervisor! She's so stupid! She must not treat me unfairly! I could kill her! (Followed by: "I shouldn't have blown up like that.")
People you supervise are goofing-off and trying to get away with murder.	Excessive anger at yourself for letting them get away with it. Rage at the Goofers.	How can they goof-off like this when I treat them so well? What ungrateful bastards they are! But maybe I'm too lenient with them, as I absolutely shouldn't be! What an ineffective person I am. It's all my fault!

Your Practice Sheet for Exercise 6A: Discovering Your Emotional and Behavioral Overreactions and Your Irrational Thinking About Your Job, Business, or Profession

Specific Situation	Your Emotional and Behavioral Overreactions	Your Irrational Thinking at That Time

Sample Practice Sheet for Exercise 6B: Changing Your Irrational Thinking About Your Job, Business, or Profession

Irrational Beliefs	Challenging and Disputing My Irrational Beliefs
I'm just no good at this, and I'll never be able to do better. I *have to* improve or I'll never keep a job. This is really awful!	I'm not perfect, but I'm getting better. I *can* do better if I keep trying. I don't *have to* do better. I'd like to. If I don't do better, it doesn't mean I'll get fired. It's unfortunate, but its not awful and horrible! Just very uncomfortable!
That lousy supervisor! She's so stupid! She *must not* treat me this unfairly! I could kill her! (Followed by: "I shouldn't be angry and so talkative.")	The supervisor unjustly criticized me, and that's bad, but it doesn't make her a rotten person. She's wrong in treating me this way, but she's a fallible human who has the right to be wrong. I'm not thrilled by her behavior, but I don't hate her as a person. I can discuss this with her without blowing my top.
How can they goof-off like this when I treat them so well? What ungrateful bastards! But maybe I'm too easy on them, when I *should not* be! What an ineffective person I am!	They *are* goofing-off. I resent it, but they are not total bastards for doing so. I *will* collar them on this. If I am acting weakly, then I'd better stop acting that way—but I'm not a total weakling if I don't stop. Let me see now how I can act more strongly.

Your Practice Sheet for Exercise 6B: Changing Your Irrational
Thinking About Your Job, Business, or Profession

Irrational Beliefs	Challenging and Disputing My Irrational Beliefs

Chapter 7

Spouses: The Ultimate Button-Pushers

Marriages are probably the toughest relationships of all to keep alive, healthy, and happy. Sometimes the roots go back to the very start. So many spouses begin with great expectations of how the other person is or will be. That's understandable, because you both may be passionately in love, and therefore not seeing the other person entirely accurately. And that's OK!

The real measure of marital success, however, comes when you have to work out the differences, conflicts, problems, and disagreements that inevitably arise. *How* you two go about resolving the differences of opinion, values, wants, preferences, and priorities is the critical factor. If you or your spouse can't or won't discuss them, if feelings are too easily hurt, if one of you is extremely defensive, these are the real problems.

If one spouse awfulizes about a problem, or shoulds on the other, or rationalizes and cons to avoid or justify or defend an action, that's deadly. Problems, conflicts, differences, and disagreements will always exist in any relationship. Fine! But if, in the process of resolving them, spouses are defensive, controlling, argumentative, manipulative, and nasty (or unassertive, avoidant, evasive, or indifferent), then somebody's buttons *have* been pushed, and at least one of them probably is awfulizing, shoulding, or rationalizing.

Very often, people *gradually* lose their love, liking, or respect for the spouse. It just seems to atrophy. Actually, *we let it atrophy*; we let it die away from neglect. Either we don't deal with the real concerns, or we give up trying. And each time we give up, we lose a little more love, liking, or respect. Some spouses look like they're just plain bored with each other (watch them eating together in a restaurant— it's like one's on Mars and the other on Venus); they're just going through the motions, putting in their time. Maybe they get their real pleasures and stimulations at work, or through the kids or hobbies or friends—or lovers. That's not good enough!

Leo Buscaglia listed, in a brief article in (believe it or not) *Bride Magazine*, the five factors essential for a good relationship. We'd like to restate them here, adding some comments of our own about each one.

Factor 1: The first factor is *communication*. Now, that seems pretty obvious—but we really liked the way he described what *he* meant by communication. As long as you are willing and able to *discuss* the issues (as opposed to fight, debate, defensively argue, or grenade-lob), you have a chance for resolution. If you are really just fighting with each other, you are not communicating—and, when communication ends, the relationship atrophies.

Factor 2: Second, do you have *a sense of humor?* Buscaglia does *not* mean you must walk in the door each night with a new joke ("Did you hear the one about the salesman and three chickens...?"). He means *do not take yourself too seriously.* Are you able to laugh at your own sensitivities, pomposities, and mountainous molehills? Do you always have to have it your way (á la Burger King)? Is everything you say terribly important and always right? Is your ego involved *too much* in what you do? Do you place too much importance on what others think (image versus substance)? Do you try *too hard* to impress?

I (A.L.) once saw *Gone With the Wind* and *Cat on a Hot Tin Roof* in two consecutive days. Scarlett O'Hara (throughout) and "Maggie the Cat" (in the beginning) were great examples of what I'm talking about—and so were Rhett Butler, Big Daddy, his wife, both his sons, and their whole family! They were all caught up at different times with taking themselves too seriously, and consequently led miserable lives then. You do not have to emulate them! But you also don't have to go to the other extreme and diminish your wants and preferences and opinions, and put yourself down. The balancing point is in the middle!

Self-confidence and humility are what we're talking about. Coach John Wooden (of UCLA basketball fame) is famous for saying, "It's what you learn after you know it all that really counts." Radio personality Paul Harvey has said, "The number of people at your funeral will be a function of the weather that day." Now, that's humility!

Factor 3: Commitment is next. Are you really, truly committed to this relationship, or are you just *there?* The oft-quoted analogy to a ham-and-egg breakfast captures the difference between being "sort of" involved and real commitment: The chicken is involved, the pig is committed. Commitment means that you regularly put out your best effort to make that relationship the very finest it can be. It may work out or it may not—but in either case you can honestly say you consistently gave it your best shot.

Frankly, we believe that our society has developed a tolerance for minimal commitment in relationships. Extramarital relationships abound, and it seems old-fashioned to be concerned about that fact. We *don't* believe that everyone *ought* to be married. All kinds of relationships work for different people, and the more options available, the better. But if you *do* make a monogamous marital commitment, it is important either to really keep it, or perhaps to end the relationship after a good, honest try. People rationalize, however, and find excuses for their uncommitted behavior in a thousand different ways—but it all just doesn't float.

There are lots of reasons (besides loss of love) why people break their marital commitments. Some people keep trying to prove they are still attractive and desirable, as though that makes them OK (fear of rejection). Others insensitively demand what *they* want regardless of the effects on others. Still others—those with low frustration tolerance—find it difficult to diligently work on the complexities of an intimate relationship, and run away (that's easier). Sometimes violations of marital commitments are also a result of an absence of integrity, which is rationalized with a variety of cons and justifications.

Minimal commitment can manifest itself in many other ways: spending little time together, poor communication, minimal sharing, neutral corners, putting each other down, boredom, manipulation, and so on. We have seen so many people who started their relationship with high hopes and excited enthusiasm, only to allow it to atrophy gradually. Keeping a relationship alive takes effort (*not* drudgery) and attention. Relationships do *not* sustain themselves. It's up to the partners to maintain that commitment attitudinaly, emotionally, and behaviorally every single day, one day at a time.[14] That's not to say that conflicts don't arise, or that friction never exists. The commitment is to resolution, communication, and respect. It's *how* you treat each other daily that defines your real commitment.

Factor 4: Buscaglia's fourth factor in successful relationships is *flexibility*. It's fine to have lots of ideas, opinions, and reactions; in fact, the more the better. But can you *listen* to the other side? Can you take a different perspective from the one you started with, when yours doesn't hold up under examination? Do you hold onto your position defensively because it's more important to be right? Can you bend, compromise, give in *sometimes?* Can you *discuss* an issue without it's becoming a debate (is too/is not; did too/did not/; are too/am not)? Does the tone of most of your disagreements take a right/wrong, good/bad, OK/not OK tone, so that everything is dichotomously black or white? Or do you seek out the various valid points being made, and work toward a mutually acceptable understanding?

Factor 5: Lastly, do you *love and respect* each other? Do you care *for and about* each other, and show it daily?

Terry Paulson, a colleague of mine, tells a story about a TV show like "The Newlywed Game" but for couples who have been together

---

[14]The unfortunately popular TV show "Married ... With Children" is supposedly an exaggerated satire on the too-good-to-be-true "Ozzie and Harriet" and "Leave It to Beaver" types of family shows. We doubt that anyone predicted the extent to which viewers would genuinely identify it as being closer to their real world.

for over 20 years. The game-winning question to the woman was: "How often in the last six months has your husband said, 'I love you'?" She immediately answered, with great certainty, "Zero." The moderator of the show laughed, but went on. The husbands were brought back in to see if they could match their spouse's answers. When this woman's husband was asked the question, he also immediately answered "Zero." They won the game! After a moment of celebration, the moderator said, "I just have to ask you something. You mean you've never said 'I love you' once in six months?" The wife said, "He hasn't told me in 20 years." The husband said, "Yup—I said to my wife, the day we were married, 'I love you', and if I ever change my mind, I'll let you know." We hear so many people (typically men, but not exclusively) say, "She knows I love her; I don't have to *say* it." Bull! If you want to keep the relationship alive, you'd better say it OFTEN—and mean it, too!

Equally important is respect. Do you put each other down (subtly or overtly) with a look of disgust or disapproval, a sarcastic or demeaning tone, a snide comment, or just indifference or disinterest? You can easily should on your spouse with a look or a tone, as well as with the actual words you speak.

Attention to the preceding five factors espoused by Leo Buscaglia will go a long way toward strengthening your relationship. But they don't just happen miraculously, do they? Actually, most of us *would* like to act these five ways naturally, spontaneously—but, instead, we indulge in nutty thinking that gets directly in the way of our initial inclinations. We indulge in awfulizing, shoulding, and rationalizing. We worry too much about what others think of us, so we either hold back our feelings and opinions, or we always have to win. (But these approaches are based on insecurity.)

If you *have* to be in control by putting the other person down; if you often criticize or (the opposite) are afraid to disagree, do you see what that does to communication? Look at Archie and Edith! It's either cut off, or it becomes a debate. If you are fearful about rejection, won't you often take yourself too seriously, and fail even to have a sense of humor as a coverup? And what do fear of rejection and failure, low frustration tolerance, and blame do to commitments?

These disturbances often make it seem *easier* to run away than to face your commitments and give them an honest try. But is it *really* easier?

How can you be flexible and discuss issues and see the other person's side when you're too busy worrying about what he or she thinks of you, or are fearing failure, or are indulging in LFT or blame? And how can you love and respect someone else (or yourself) when you are awfulizing, shoulding, and rationalizing about these nutty, screwball beliefs? It's virtually impossible!

Leo Buscaglia's five factors are great outcome goals. *How* to attain them, however, requires *changing* your thinking in specific situations, so that you *don't* indulge in awfulizing, shoulding, or rationalizing, but instead think *realistic* preferences.

We've selected a few typical situations wherein you might overreact and allow someone to push your buttons—and here they are.

The Public Stiletto

You (let's say a woman) are at a meeting of parents who are high-school boosters. The spokesperson asks for assistance with the next year's football program. As soon as you volunteer to chair the group, your husband—loud enough for others to hear and somewhat condescendingly—says, "Honey, you don't know a thing about selling advertising and doing layouts. Leave this to somebody with good business sense. You're probably in over your head." Let's assume you really let him push your buttons.

Step 1: How am I inappropriately feeling and acting?

Furious, extremely upset, mortified; say something really nasty back to him in front of the group, leaving an awkward moment for everyone, and uncertainty about your chairing the committee; get him good when you get home (better yet, in the car!).

Step 2: What am I irrationally thinking to make myself excessively anxious, angry, depressed, or guilty?

a: What am I thinking about myself?

"What if he's right? What if I *am* trying to be more than I am? What if I took the job and really blew it? That would be *terrible!* [I

should be able to do this job as well as, or better than, anyone else!]
Everyone heard what he said. I'm so embarrassed, I just want to die!"

b: What am I thinking about others?

"How dare he embarrass me and put me down like that? If he
has to have such negative opinions, he *should* just keep his mouth
shut! Why does he always have to put me down? He's so insensitive!
He wouldn't like it at all if I said something like that to him, that
jackass! What if they don't want me as chairperson now?"

c: What am I thinking about the situation?

"What should I do now? If I withdraw, I've quit—and if I push
it, they may not want me. This is a mess, and it's all his fault. [Things
should not be this difficult!]"

Step 3: How can I challenge and dispute my irrational thinking?

"It's obvious he doesn't believe I can do this job—but do I
need his approval? No! Is it really devastating and mortifying that he
embarrassed me in the group? Only if I make it so! *Should* I
embarrass him back; does he *deserve* it? Would that help the
situation? No! Do I *have to* have the group's support, and *must* I be
able to guarantee that I will succeed? No! If I do take the job, *must* I
prove that I am competent? No!"

*Step 4: What realistic preferences can I substitute for my irrational
thinking?*

"I'd *like* him to have more confidence in my abilities, but
he doesn't *have to*. I'm disappointed and concerned—but not
horrified—that he doesn't. I'd also like him to keep such negative
comments to *us*, if he feels strongly enough to want to suggest them
at all. I especially don't like the condescension in his voice. I want
him to treat me with dignity and respect, whatever his opinion. If he
doesn't, I'm not going to attack him or lose my composure. I can
express my concerns, let him know how I feel, and talk with him
without fighting. I can let him know I am displeased and sorry
without overreacting."

If you instantly see red and make yourself *overly* angry, you may let
him have it in front of everyone, just as he did to you: "*You* may think
I'm in over my head, but that doesn't mean other people do. Why do
you always have to act so superior? You're no genius, but you love to

put everyone else down. What are you, jealous? Maybe you're afraid I might succeed and show *you* up."

Even if your comments are accurate, it won't do you much good to have a public quarrel. On the other hand, if you *rationalize* what he says, you might decide that you aren't up to the job, that maybe he's right, that he really means well—and withdraw your offer to chair the group.

If, however, you are thinking realistic preferences, you may say right then and there, but privately (with no sarcastic tone), "You are entitled to your opinion, but I believe I'll do a fine job and I'd like to give it a try." Then go on to renew your offer to chair the committee. Later, also in private, you might say, "When you loudly discouraged me from being chairperson by saying I was in over my head, I think you undermined my credibility with the group and you put me down. I really don't like that. We may not agree on whether I can do the job, but I would much prefer that we talk about these things privately and without your sounding so condescending." He may become defensive or he may admit he was out of line. Either way, you can continue to *discuss* the issue without getting *overly* upset. It is certainly legitimate to feel hurt and disappointed about what he did, but you can express that without overreacting yourself. It's not easy, but you can do it!

Don't Tread on Me

Your spouse says, in a very appropriate way, that she'd like to talk with you about what she thinks is a defensive, sarcastic, argumentative manner on your part when you disagree on issues. You immediately get defensive, sarcastic, and argumentative about it.

Step 1: How am I inappropriately feeling and acting?

Threatened and defensive. You demand specific examples, and explain away any that are offered. You counterattack with criticisms of her, and accuse her of being overly sensitive and thinskinned. You agree to nothing, and end up walking away and sulking.

Step 2: What am I irrationally thinking to make myself excessively anxious, angry, depressed, guilty, or behave inappropriately?

a: What am I thinking about myself?

"I'm not defensive at all, and I won't be criticized for it. I just speak the truth, and that's tough to hear sometimes. Too bad! I must not be criticized else I'm not really a strong person!"

b: What am I thinking about the others?

"She just doesn't like losing all our arguments. If she cant take the heat, that's her problem. She's trying to make me into some kind of wimp. I hate it when she exaggerates and then tries to make me out to be a creep. Get off my back! What a horrible nag she is!"

c: What am I thinking about the situation?

"This is a joke. I don't need this aggravation [and it shouldn't exist]. I don't deserve this attack!"

Step 3: How can I challenge and dispute my irrational thinking?

"Why is it *awful* if she's criticizing me? Must I always be *right?* Does she *have to* get off my back? Do I have to get defensive now and attack her? Where is the evidence that this aggravation *shouldn't* exist and that I don't deserve this?"

Step 4: How can I substitute realistic preferences for my irrational thoughts?

"I'd *prefer* not to be criticized, but when I am, it's not awful and I don't have to be defensive. I can discuss it and agree or disagree without being harsh or nasty. Honestly, I'd *like* to be able to continue being sarcastic and argumentative, because it works great in disagreements, but *it would be better* to knock that off, since it doesn't help our relationship in the long run. I don't need to protect myself that way. I'd *like* to win every disagreement, but I don't have to at any cost."

This kind of thinking helps us to question some of our "natural" reactions (defensiveness) that are pretty dysfunctional and only cause more trouble. Realistic preferences also provide an alternative way to think about the situation without feeling threatened. *Nobody* likes to be criticized, but *some* people believe that being wrong is a major danger to be avoided and denied at all costs. Realistic preferences challenge those underlying screwball beliefs, and substitute much healthier thoughts. At that point we can admit to valid criticisms, and discuss calmly those with which we disagree.

If you awfulize and should on your spouse, you will likely act defensively and be sarcastic, the very things she's talking about. If you rationalize, you might wind up justifying your behavior, or dismissing her. But, if you think realistic preferences, as in Step 4, you would say something like; "You're right, I don't need to be defensive or sarcastic. Sometimes I just do it without even thinking about it, but that's no excuse. I'll work on not being defensive or sarcastic, even if I'm highly displeased with something you say or do." Then really *work* on not being defensive, by *changing* your thinking next time!

This very same situation of dealing with criticism could also be *reversed*. Let's say *you* express what you think is a valid criticism of your spouse, and *you* get a defensive response, and *that leads you to get extremely upset*. (Also, let's say you're a woman.) See how you could be part of the problem, even though you didn't start it.

The Old Switcheroo: Putting It Back on You

You believe it is important to be able to *discuss* conflicts and disagreements with your spouse. When you do, though, he invariably becomes defensive, sarcastic, and adversarial. It's no longer a discussion, but a debate he has to win. You try to talk with him about his aggressive manner and he says, "See, here we go again. Why can't you just ignore my sarcasm? Why do you have to make a big deal out of everything? Not everybody is perfect, like you. I have feelings, and that's how I express them. You just want me to be like you, a robot; you're always trying to change me or control me. Besides, why do you always have to talk, talk, talk about everything? Lighten up— you're always so analytical."

Step 1: How am I inappropriately feeling and acting?

Shifting among extreme anger and hurt, upsetness, and depression; torn between blowing up, giving up, or crying.

Step 2: What am I irrationally thinking to make myself excessively anxious, angry, depressed, guilty, or behave poorly?

a: What am I thinking about myself?

"I don't have to take this baloney! What a manipulator! I've *got to* stand right up to him. I *can't stand it* when he twists everything around and tries to put it all back on me!"

b: What am I thinking about the others?

"What a jerk! He's driving me nuts [as he *shouldn't!*]. He's so defensive, he can't hear one thing that's critical, even if it's true. He's so immature, he's just a big baby! He's just blowing up so he can hide behind the smokescreen. I can see right through him. He's not going to get away with it this time, that stinker!"

c: What am I thinking about the situation?

"This is *so* frustrating! How can it get any better if we can't even talk about what's going on? It's hopeless! It's not fair, and it's all his fault!"

Step 3: How can I challenge and dispute my irrational thoughts?

"He's doing the very thing I'm trying to talk with him about right now [being defensive], but do I *have to* get overly upset myself, attack him back, and have a fight? No! He *is* argumentative, but does that make him a jerk, a worm, or a big baby? No! Can I stand it when he tries to twist things around? Yes! Is it natural for me to be upset in this situation? Yes! Do I *have to* overreact? No!"

Step 4: How can I substitute realistic preferences for my irrational thinking?

"I'd *like* him to be more willing to discuss our disagreements and conflicts without being sarcastic and hostile, but I don't need him to be. I *want* him to treat me with more respect, and not try to manipulate me or twist my words around, but I *can* stand it if he manipulates and twists. He *is* presently being sarcastic, and I'm seriously concerned about that—but it's not *awful, terrible,* or *horrible* and I don't have to blow up or get dysfunctional myself. I don't like the way he is acting, but I don't have to act that way myself, or give up. I can continue to tell him how I feel, and say that I believe it's very important for us to be able to discuss sensitive issues without fighting."

Even this realistic set of thoughts doesn't solve the fundamental problem, but it does keep *you* from becoming part of it (by either blowing up or giving up). If, after really trying to have a discussion, you still get sarcasm, defensiveness, and counterattacks, then you can frankly decide just how important this aspect of your relationship is, and whether you are willing to stay in it without improvement. Whatever you decide, you can live without the bitterness of shoulding on him or yourself.

If we wanted to speculate on *why* your mate is behaving in this sarcastic way, there are hundreds of "psychological" explanations. Some people (including therapists) love to indulge in such interpretive speculations:

1. He's afraid to *discuss* issues because he'll probably "lose" a logical discussion, and that would mean he's stupid.
2. He's competitive, controlling, fundamentally insecure, can't ever be wrong, and must be lacking in self-esteem and self-worth.
3. He's a mean, nasty creep who enjoys being difficult.
4. His parents didn't toilet-train him properly.
5. He has unresolved conflicts with authority figures.
6. He's making life miserable to justify in his own mind why he's fooling around with someone else.
7. He's got a lot of other problems on his mind—*ad infinitum*.

Frankly, Scarlett!

Although there often are underlying causes of conflicts in relationships, if you don't exercise self-control and refuse to let your partner push your buttons, you'll never be able to discuss what they are, or even come close to resolving them. You'll be too busy lobbing grenades. Besides, the "underlying" problems that exacerbate this situation are most probably fear of rejection and failure, LFT, and blaming by both of you.

In a scenario similar to the one just described, you (again, a woman) might respond by rationalizing. Here's how *that* could go.

Maybe It's Me

Step 1: How am I inappropriately feeling and acting?
          Extremely guilty, confused, and anxious. Giving up, apologizing for being a crab, and going into the other room and crying.

Step 2: What am I irrationally thinking to make myself feel excessively anxious, angry, depressed, or guilty?

    a: What am I irrationally thinking about myself?

    "Maybe I *am* too demanding. Who am I to try to change him Maybe I expect too much. I'm probably just in a bad mood. I should just take the bad with the good."

    b: What am I irrationally thinking about the others?

    "He's not all that bad. He's probably got a million other worries; he doesn't need *my* problems on top of them. He's right about putting me down for being so analytic."

    c: What am I irrationally thinking about the situation?

    "I'm sorry I brought it up at all. Now he'll probably be upset all night. Why didn't I just keep my big mouth shut? It's easier to avoid this situation than to try to do something about it."

Step 3: How can I challenge and dispute my rationalizations?

    "Am I really too demanding, or am I making a reasonable request to discuss our disagreement? Is it true that I expect too much? Doesn't he have a right to his feelings, *and* do I have a right to ask him to change his behavior? Is it really better to just give up and avoid the situation?"

Step 4: How can I substitute realistic preferences for my rationalizations?

    "I'd like him to be more willing to discuss disagreements without being sarcastic, but if he isn't, it's a pain in the neck but not *awful*. I'd *like* to talk with him about his defensiveness, without his being defensive. If he is still argumentative, that's frustrating and I'm seriously concerned about it, but I don't have to run away, give up, or talk myself out of it. I am committed to continuing to express my concerns without blaming him or myself. I am concerned about how he feels toward me, but I am not willing to avoid this just because he might not like what I am saying."

In this case, instead of keeping yourself from blowing up, you are giving yourself permission to express your opinions and concerns, as opposed to conning yourself into silence or blaming yourself for your mate's defensiveness.

If you did awfulize and should on him in this situation, you might defensively snap back and insinuate several nasty reasons why he's being so argumentative—and the fight is on its way. If you rationalize, you might just shut up, give up, walk away, and be miserable. If you are thinking realistic preferences, however, you might say, "I know it's not pleasant to talk about disagreements, but we don't have to fight over them. When you get defensive or sarcastic, it keeps us from being able to stay focused on the problem itself so that we can resolve it. I know you have feelings. So do I. I think we can express them without being sarcastic and defensive. What do you think?"

If you get a cooperative response, great! You're on your way to working it out. If, however, he continues to be defensive and sarcastic right there, you can say something like, "When you keep being sarcastic even now, it seems like you would rather fight than get along, and I'm seriously concerned about that. I don't want to fight with you."

If it just gets worse, you could end it with a comment like: "This isn't working right now. I'd like to stop. I think we have a real problem, and I don't want to ignore it. It's important that we still get along, even when we disagree." You didn't get any agreement or cooperation, but you *did* keep yourself from overreacting in the face of continuous resistance, and that's good for you. Remember, if you are only acting cool on the outside, but inside you are seething, you probably are allowing some awfulizing and shoulding to sneak into your thoughts.

You can keep from burning up inside by *consistently* thinking realistic preferences as in Step 4! If you continue to confront your mate's behavior in an appropriate manner, you may just get improvement. If you don't see any change in spite of your efforts, you will have to decide how serious the problem is, and what action is most appropriate: staying (but minimizing conflict situations), seeking counseling for both of you, or leaving—if it's that bad. You know, however, that you gave it a really good try, and you did not overreact or let him push your buttons in the process.

The Green-eyed Monster

Your wife has been gone for several days on a business trip (national sales meeting). Although you have talked each night, you tried reaching her several other times but got no answer—and you know what can go on "on the side" at meetings like these. She walks in the door, dog-tired from a long day and a delayed flight, but you have been building up for several days. If you've pushed your own buttons, here's one way it might go from there.

Step 1: How am I inappropriately feeling and acting?

Extremely jealous, anxious, hurt, angry, insecure. I greet her with something like: "Well, did you have a good trip? How many salesmen hit on you this time? I tried to call you at the hotel three times and got no answer. Running all around town? Don't worry, the kids and I did fine by ourselves. Tell the truth—don't you really enjoy it when all these guys come on to you at these meetings?"

Step 2: What am I irrationally thinking to make myself excessively anxious, angry, depressed, guilty, or behave inappropriately?

a: What am I thinking about myself?

"What if she isn't as attracted to me as she is to those hotshots? What if she thinks I'm boring? That would be awful! It would be terrible! What a loser!"

b: What am I thinking about others?

"I know what those sleazeballs are like. They'll hustle some-one just for the challenge—their egos need it. And they're so smooth and sneaky. What if she's attracted to one of these guys and goes along? What if she isn't really faithful? What if she likes the flattery and attention? What if she starts it! What if she's out there looking around and figures I'll never find out? How do I know for sure how she feels and what she's doing? [What a dumb, trusting jerk I'd be! What a fool!]"

c: What am I thinking about the situation?

"It's a perfect scene for sex. Nice hotel, lavish dinners, lots of free time, everybody's celebrating their success, they can have a fling and go home safely, lots of drinking, a hotel full of con men! How revolting!"

Step 3: How can I challenge and dispute my irrational thinking?

"The situation *is* potentially dangerous, and some people in the group will probably exploit it. But is there any reason to believe that *she* would exploit it? Does getting upset and worrying about it keep it from happening? Will worry help me to enjoy these several days? Am I really a loser or fool if I trust my wife, even if she or others violate that trust? Am *I* a jerk if she or others think they got away with something?"

Step 4: How can I substitute realistic preferences for my thinking?

        "I'd like her to take our marriage vows seriously and to not want to 'fool around' at any meeting. I would prefer that nobody else flirt with her, but I can't guarantee that, and I am seriously concerned about it. I don't like it, but it wouldn't be *awful* and I *could* stand it. It would be better to trust her, and let her know that I am uncomfortable and that I will handle my discomfort. Unfortunately, it's quite normal for these men to be after her; she's an attractive woman. Too bad, but it is. I don't like it, but I *can* stand it."

Thinking like this will make the three days without your wife much more livable, and you will not build yourself up to such a point where you make jealous, nutty comments when she comes through the door. You are easily able to admit that you are worried about the realities of such a situation, and that you would like reassurance and confirmation of her commitment to you.

You might say to her, sometime *after* she's settled down a bit herself, something like this: "I'm really glad you're home. I missed you. I've been worried and upset that you might be fooling around at the conference. I know that lots of people hit on each other at these things, and I know I can't stop them from trying. I just want to know that you didn't encourage anyone, and that you didn't respond. I'd like some reassurance that you're committed to me, and that nothing happened." Some people might think that this makes you sound like an insecure wimp, and that you should never express such vulnerable feelings. That's baloney. We *all* have these doubts sometimes, and it's just fine to ask for—but not *demand*—that kind of reassurance. All you can do is ask, and trust her answer until you have *real* reasons to believe otherwise. This will save you a very large load of misery.

There's another, more intense level of thinking that might also go on: "It really *would* be awful, terrible, horrible, the end of the world, if my wife *did* have an affair at the meeting." Of course, it would be one of the most serious moments in your life, but even that doesn't have to be as devastating as we can sometimes make it. You might possibly end the relationship, or do whatever you think is right, but you do *not* have to devastate or immobilize yourself.

Admittedly (assuming you genuinely love your wife), you would likely feel deeply hurt and legitimately angry—and that might last for some time. But we have seen many people who destroy themselves as they persist in making themselves devastated, bitter, enraged, and depressed. Using the techniques presented in this book, people learn how to take control of even the most serious of emotional events, and minimize (not maximize) their responses to them.

After writing the example just discussed we realized that this situation—as is true of many others—can also be approached from the *other* person's perspective. What if you were the wife, just back from the trip, and were greeted at the door with several sarcastic, snotty comments insinuating that you had sex with "other men"—but you were perfectly innocent of anything, and merely worn out from work and travel? What could you do to keep from overreacting?

Step 1: How am I inappropriately feeling and acting?

Extremely angry and disgusted. Shouting a few nasty comments back, storming out of the room, and going to bed enraged.

Step 2: What am I thinking to make myself excessively anxious, angry, depressed, guilty, or behave inappropriately?

a: What am I thinking about myself?

"I don't have to listen to these ridiculous insinuations. I've been working my tail off, and I have to come home to *this?* I should always behave so well that he never ever suspects me of fooling around."

b: What am I thinking about the others?

"He's got no right to be accusing me of anything! His petty jealousy is maddening. He's so insecure [and he *shouldn't* be]. He's trying to make me feel guilty because I have a really good job! Maybe he accused me of this stuff because that's what *he* does on *his* business trips! That creep!"

c: What am I thinking about the situation?

"This is stupid: I'm going to bed. I don't need this. I can't stand it?"

Step 3: How can I challenge and dispute my irrational thinking?

"He is wrongly accusing me of fooling around, of flirting and enjoying it, and he's being hostile and sarcastic—and I don't like it. But why *shouldn't* he be wrong, when he *is*. Is he really a creep, or just a human who is now acting creepily? Where is it written that he *must* never be jealous? Do I *have* to put him in his place, and not even listen to or discuss this stuff?"

Step 4: How can I substitute realistic preferences for my irrational thinking?

"I want him to trust me, and be happy to see me when I get home—but, as a fallible human, he can easily be wrong and untrusting. He's certainly not a worm, in spite of his dislikable behavior. I am disappointed that he is insecure about my loyalty to him! I don't *have to* put him in his place, though honestly I would like to, right now. I am committed to talking with him (not fighting) about his concerns, and I will ask him to talk with me without making accusations or insinuations. I will not get myself overly upset and let him push my buttons. I want him to trust me, and I want him to tell me how he feels without attacking me or trying to make me feel guilty. I *can* tell him how I'd like him to talk to me about these feelings."

If you do think realistic preferences, instead of tearing into him you would say something like: "I know you're upset, but when you attack me and imply that I'm guilty of doing something wrong, I don't even want to discuss it with you. I don't want to fight with you the minute I get home. Tell me what's bothering you, and let me respond. We can discuss this without fighting." You may or may not get a cooperative response, but you certainly did keep your cool under heavy fire and miserable conditions. The way to go!

What a Dummy

You typically are responsible for paying the bills in the family. You write a check for the property taxes, and hold on to it until the last day (to save the interest, of course). You ask your spouse to be sure to mail it on the way to work on that crucial day, or you will have to pay a large penalty. You leave it on the table by the door, so it will be easy to see. You return that evening and find the letter still sitting there, untouched. Your spouse comes in the door a few minutes later, expecting a big hug and a kiss. You completely lose it.

Step 1: How am I inappropriately feeling and acting?

Extremely upset and angry. The minute my spouse walks in the door, I say, "You forgot to mail the damn check! Now we're going to have a $300 penalty. I put it right in front of your nose this morning. For crying out loud, what do I need to do—tie a bell around your neck to remind you to think?"

Step 2: What am I thinking to make myself excessively anxious, angry, depressed, guilty, or behave inappropriately?

a: What am I thinking about myself?

"I did *my* job; I went out of my way to get that check out on time, and it was still screwed up. I can't win for trying. I *should have* known he would forget to mail it! I *should* have gone out and mailed it myself. What an idiot I am!"

b: What am I thinking about the others?

"How could he be so stupid? Where is he, on Mars? This was not a toughie, and he *still* messed it up, that dummy!"

c: What am I thinking about the situation?

"This is just great! Now we're out 300 bucks because of some stupid mistake. Damn! After all I did to make it right. Things *shouldn't* be this bad!"

Step 3: How can I challenge and dispute my irrational thinking?

"Should I really have known he would forget—am I an idiot? He forgot this important task, but does that make him an incompetent dummy deserving of my wrath? Will my getting extremely upset about it be of any help, or will it solve the problem?"

Step 4: How can I substitute realistic preferences for my irrational thinking?

"It would have been better if the check had been mailed on time, but I did my best, and that was all I could do. It wasn't mailed, and that's going to cost us a good chunk of money. That's frustrating and I am annoyed, but it's not awful unless I make it so. My spouse acted quite forgetfully, but he's hardly a dummy. I can express my frustration without being obnoxious. I can be annoyed yet convey my serious concern without using the howitzers. I don't have to be overly upset to get my point across."

You can then let your spouse know how frustrated you are without being nasty, and you will also reduce the chances of a defensive response. Even when people know they're wrong, when it's pointed out to them in a putdown manner they often will be defensive—not just because of being wrong, but also because of the way the complaint was conveyed. Now, to criticize someone's *behavior* without putting the *person* down is an art, not a science. You might say, "I went out of my way to remind you to mail that bill, and you still didn't do it. Now it's going to cost us an extra $300, and that's really frustrating." You are still being critical of your spouse's neglectful action, but there is no putdown. You may still get a defensive response, but you didn't (and still don't need to) go for the jugular.

If you do get a defensive response, or an excuse, you can respond with "I know we all forget things, but this one was really important. Maybe we can figure out how to make sure this doesn't happen again." You don't have to blast away; you can be frustrated and still show some empathy. If you were awfulizing, or shoulding on your spouse, it would be very difficult to stay in control. Thinking realistic preferences allows you to stay in control, inside and out.

In Chapter 3's Exercises section you'll find some more situations wherein you can see how differently you could react, depending on how you are thinking. In that set of examples, you can see the difference between what awfulizing, shoulding, and rationalizing look like, and how differently someone would behave, depending on that person's thinking. Remember, these are not the only ways you could think or behave if you were in the situation; they are intended to be examples of *each* type of thinking and resulting behaviors. You might even speculate on how *you* would think in the situation, and which category it would fit into: awfulizing, shoulding, rationalizing, or realistic preferences. Check out some of the examples that might be relevant to your world.

The cases in this chapter and in the Exercises are real ones. They may be similar to your own situation, but not exactly the same. They have been offered here so you can picture and understand how the four steps can work in real life, and to show how different your behavior might be, depending on how you are thinking, in a given situation.

Now, it's time to take one or two of your own real-life situations wherein you have overreacted (or are presently overreacting), and walk yourself through the four steps—to see how you can better direct and control the way you respond. Practice is the key! Use the practice sheets in Chapter 5's Exercises section to guide you through the four steps. The more you use these steps, the better and more quickly will you be able to apply them and thus reduce your overreaction. After a short time of practice, you will not be "correcting" your thinking remedially, but—even better—you'll *think realistic preferences* in the first place. Go for it!

EXERCISES

Exercise 7A: Changing Your Emotional and Behavioral Overreactions and Your Irrational Thinking in Situations Involving Relationships and Spouses

This exercise will give you practice in discovering and changing your emotional and behavioral overreactions and your irrational thinking in situations involving relationships and spouses. First think of specific pertinent situations in which you tend to overreact and then identify what you are irrationally thinking at that time.

Sample Practice Sheet for Exercise 7A: Discovering Your Emotional and Behavioral Overreactions and Your Irrational Thinking in Situations Involving Relationships and Spouses

Specific Situation	Your Emotional and Behavioral Overreactions	Your Irrational Thinking at That Time
My spouse is much nicer to other people than to me.	Anxiety and depression; jealousy; avoiding talking about the situation.	What have I done wrong? I must really be a loser! Am I really that unimportant, even to him [her]?
My lover lied to me about seeing another person.	Extreme jealousy; shock; outrage; fear; deception.	My lover doesn't care for me anymore. What did I do to be so inadequate? I can't stand it if he [she] has other interests!
My mate keeps criticizing me when I've done nothing wrong.	Anger and anxiety. I avoid my spouse.	How awful! I can't stand this kind of criticism! It's just not fair! Maybe I really am a loser!

Your Practice Sheet for Exercise 7A: Discovering Your Emotional and Behavioral Overreactions and Your Irrational Thinking in Situations Involving Relationships and Spouses

Specific Situation	Your Emotional and Behavioral Overreactions	Your Irrational Thinking at That Time

Sample Practice Worksheet for Exercise 7B: Changing Your Irrational
Thinking in Situations Involving Relationships and Spouses

Irrational Beliefs	Challenging and Disputing My Irrational Beliefs
What have I done wrong? I must really be a loser. Am I really that unimportant, even to him [her]?	How does my mate's being much nicer to other people prove that I've done anything wrong? Even if I had done something wrong, that doesn't make me a loser. I'd better find out whether he or she really dislikes me— and, if so, change my ways. If I can never please him [her] it's still not the end of my life.
My lover doesn't care for me anymore. What did I do to be so inadequate? I can't stand it if he [she] has other interests!	Even if he [she] is seeing someone else, does that make me an inadequate person? I hate my mate's lying to me, but he [she] still has the right to do so. Although I'll never like it, I *can* stand it and deal with it.
How awful! I can't stand this kind of criticism! It's just not fair! Maybe I really am a loser!	His [her] criticism is really annoying, but why is it so awful? It isn't, and I definitely can stand it. He [she] is being unfair, but there's no law against this kind of behavior. Even if his [her] criticism is correct, that doesn't make me a loser—just somebody with failings that, I hope, I can now correct, and will try to correct.

Your Practice Worksheet for Exercise 7B: Changing Your Irrational
Thinking in Situations Involving Relationships and Spouses

Irrational Beliefs	Challenging and Disputing My Irrational Beliefs

Chapter 8

Parenting: The Penultimate Test

The first step in learning not to let your children push your buttons is to accept the fact that they can behave like real creeps. That does not mean that they *are* creeps, but that they often can act "creepily." It also does not mean that you're supposed to like it, tolerate it, or ignore it. We often see "creep-like" behavior in them, yet it never ceases to amaze us. We can get ourselves incredibly upset, angry, frustrated, agitated, uptight, and wigged out when they act creepily. And there are *so* many things we can get upset about!

They *should* have wonderful attitudes about school and grades and future careers. They *should* keep their rooms neat (clean, with no bizarre posters, signs, and "decor"), and should get along beautifully with brothers and sisters. They *should* act in a mature, thoughtful, responsible, sensitive, loving, positive manner toward everyone and everything. They *should* not only have the right attitudes, but they *should* also *be* A+ students (in honors classes), three-letter athletes, band members, artists, drama club presidents, and computer whizzes—*and* not get into sex (prematurely) or drugs and violence (ever). They *should* receive awards for "most popular," be Homecoming King or Queen, "most likely to succeed," and (in general) nicest person in the world. Actually, some of us would settle for passing grades and no criminal record!

It's when they do *not* think, feel, and act as we know they *should*

149

that we have the potential to make ourselves overly upset. Each individual event may not be that big a deal, but after the 4,000th time you see dirty dishes, and glasses with fuzzy, multicolored fungi left all over the house, it can become a potential blowup situation. You can have at least three main sets of thoughts about all of this—

One might be a combination of awfulizing and shoulding: "I can't stand it anymore! I think he *likes* living in a pig sty. That's it, I'm going to kill him! When is he going to grow up and take responsibility?" (Certainly never, if you *do* kill him!) This type of thinking will likely lead to a blowup and a nasty fight.

On the other hand, you might rationalize: "I might as well pick it up myself. I give up—it's too much of a hassle. What's the use of trying to get him to change?" This kind of thinking will lead both to exasperation and to reinforcement of the undesired behavior if you do it all *for* him (that's called *learned helplessness*).

The third thoughts can be realistic preferences: "I'd *like* him to pick his things up without being constantly reminded, but that consistently hasn't worked. That's really frustrating, but not *awful*. I don't need to get myself worked up."

These rational thoughts then enable you to confront him with the mess, get him to clean it up, and penalize him for not having cleaned up on his own initiative (usually by taking something away—ground him, including no use of the phone, TV, car, etc.). The success of such penalties is very much a function of *how* you say them. If you have gotten yourself all worked up ("OK, mister, this time you're gonna pay for your mess: You're grounded!"), you probably will get an argument back.

If, however, you do not upset yourself by awfulizing and shoulding, you could say something like, "Bill, you have continued to leave messes around like this one, even though we've talked to you about it repeatedly. You are grounded Friday night, and I want you to pick up these things now." Bill might respond in a million different ways (usually all negative), but let's say he whines and complains, gives excuses, and gets upset (often as a smokescreen to get you to back off). He says, "That's not fair. I didn't have time, and besides, you didn't warn me, and you didn't make Mary pick up her stuff yesterday. Why does everything have to be put away *right away?* It's like living in a furniture-store window. Geeez!" (He tries to storm away.)

At this point you don't have to escalate, but you can still be firm: "I know you don't like being grounded, but I expect you to take responsibility—and when you don't, there are real consequences. I also expect you to talk about this without overreacting or storming away." If Bill gets it together and doesn't act disrespectfully any further, wonderful. If he continues to overreact, then end the conversation and perhaps punish him for being rude, too.

How you say all this will greatly influence the response you get. If your tone of voice is sarcastic or argumentative (daring him to respond), or tentative or meek, you may get a different response than if you speak directly, honestly, and as though you clearly mean what you say, with no hesitation or putdown. Again, if you are awfulizing and shoulding, and getting yourself overly upset, it's hard not to show it in the tone of your voice, your facial expression, or your gestures. You see, if you are thinking in terms of preferences, it's easier to be direct and impactful, without all the extra provocations.

Parents can overreact to relatively minor chronic issues like the one just described, and to very serious problems (drugs, alcohol, vandalism, sexual activity, stealing, quitting school), and everything in between (fighting with brothers and sisters, breaking curfew, cutting classes, not doing chores). Certainly the more serious the event, the more strongly we tend to react—but we don't have to *overreact* to any of them.

One increasingly common parenting arrangement has its own unique potential for overreactions: stepparenting. In some cases, children are brought together as a family from two previously separate families. There are lots of different "step" arrangements, each with its own unique circumstances and dynamics. They *all* have the potential to push buttons.

The stepparent has to deal with the reality that no matter how loving and caring and giving he or she is, the children often show a different kind of love to their natural parents—even when one of them exercises visitation rights only occasionally and contributes less to the child's welfare. It can come out in subtle forms, like how you are greeted each day or talked to at dinner, or how goodnights are said, or how birthdays and holidays are handled. It's easy to feel resentful and hurt as a stepparent.

Sometimes stepparents and stepchildren are suddenly living together—often with different values, expectations, and styles. The potential for button-pushing (sometimes after an initial "honeymoon") is great. Moreover, *any* set of parents can clash over how to raise children, but it's even *more* difficult when a stepparent enters the picture after the natural parent has already been "parenting" in a particular way for some time.

Stepparents have a great potential for awfulizing ("I can't stand it when the kids treat me like an outsider!"), shoulding ("He *should* appreciate that I was the one who was there every time he was sick or in trouble or needed someone!"), or rationalizing ("Oh, it doesn't really bother me, deep down I know she probably loves me."). Stepparents can give their children enormous power to push their buttons if they don't think clearly about their expectations. Nasty fights can arise from seemingly day-to-day issues (dress, curfew, bedtime, grades) that are really battles over the underlying attitudes and reactions between stepparents and stepchildren. Few of these overreactions have to happen, and won't if you use the guidelines we have already provided. "Step" relationships are difficult under the best of circumstances—but they all can be greatly improved when everyone is thinking and feeling according to realistic preferences.

Regardless of whether you are a "natural" parent or a "step" parent, some of us have much more serious parenting problems to deal with than others. We have picked a few examples to follow that cover the gamut from small hassles (but a real pain) to very serious concerns. They are some of the most common problems cited by parents in the many workshops we have conducted with them.

This first section shows how to use the four-step process (described earlier) to change your nutty thinking. And the following Exercises section demonstrates one type of awfulizing, shoulding, rationalizing, and realistic preferences that you might think in some specific situations—and how differently you might behave as a result of each.

You might agree or disagree with the position taken in these examples. That's not the primary point, though—so we would encourage you not to focus too heavily on what you think is the "right" or "wrong" way to handle them, or the position one "should" take in these matters. You are entitled to (and responsible for) your own way to handle these situations. We're not suggesting that this is *the* way to do it.

The focus here is to show you how you can use the four-step process to exercise greater self-control, regardless of what action you choose to take. There are lots of other awfulizings, shoulds, rationalizations, and realistic preferences that you *could* think in these situations. But if you do awfulize, should, or rationalize, you will either overreact or run away from the situation, and make the practical problem of handling your kids worse. You may then indeed become part—the overly emotional part—of the problem.

The Sibs Are "at It" Again

For the 4,000th time this week (same as any other) your nine-year-old son and seven-year-old daughter are at each other's throats over something trivial. You've had a rotten week yourself, and you just came in the door.

Step 1: How am I inappropriately feeling and acting?

A typical overresponse would be to get angry and upset, but let's say, in this situation, it's gone even beyond that—to depression. I just want to crawl in a hole and get away. I feel helpless and hopeless, really oppressed by their constant bickering. I feel lost, flat, blank, out of it.

Step 2: What am I irrationally thinking to make myself excessively anxious, angry, depressed, or guilty?

a: What am I thinking about myself?

"I give up. I don't know what else I can do. I feel so helpless. I'm a failure as a parent. I *should* be able to get them to be nice to each other, so why can't I? I never should have had children. I can't take it anymore!"

    b: What am I thinking about the others?

    "They never stop or let up. They hate each other. They don't even listen to me anymore. What rotten kids! They're hopeless!"

    c: What am I thinking about the situation?

    "It's never going to get better. Day after day I have to live with this. I *can't bear* it! Some say it gets even worse later. It can't possibly!"

    Step 3: How can I challenge my irrational thinking?

    "It *is* unpleasant, and it happens a lot, but where is it written that I *can't stand it* anymore? Does the fact that they don't stop even when I yell at them make me a failure, *or* that I have failed all along in my efforts? Are *they* depressing me, or am I depressing *myself?* Does getting depressed help? Are they rotten kids, or are they behaving rottenly? When I get upset and yell, is that helping to solve the problem?"

    Step 4: What realistic preferences can I substitute for my irrational thoughts?

    "I want them to stop fighting as much, and get along more, but they don't. It's not awful, terrible, and horrible, and it is not hopeless unless I make it so. I'd like to have been more successful in dealing with this. I haven't been, though, and that's frustrating—but it's really not awful. I'm not a failure as a parent, and I can keep working on this problem. It's frustrating and annoying, but I *can* handle it. I am committed to hanging in there and not getting depressed. It's bad enough that they are acting like brats—but should I make myself depressed about it? No! I hate their bratty *behavior*. I want them to get along, and I will continue to work at that with them."

    This kind of thinking can get you out of the hopeless, helpless, depressed feelings, and also enable you to confront the kids firmly (without blowing up again), perhaps by saying something like:

    "I want you to stop fighting with each other. Who started it or what happened is not as important as *not fighting*. If you have a problem, you are to work it out without yelling or teasing, or being nasty. As a last resort, if either of you continues to be obnoxious after you've tried several times, you can either stop playing with each other or come to me—but I don't want to hear any *whining* or *tattling*. Tell me specifically what is happening and what you want from me.

"I also want you to treat each other decently, especially when you're frustrated or irritated. If you continue to fight, you will *both* be punished, because either of you could stop it by either talking decently or leaving. Don't wait for me to say 'Stop it!' anymore, because I'm not going to do that. I want *you* to take responsibility for seeing that it doesn't happen. I'm not going to play referee anymore: I'm going to take away the things you like if you continue to fight.

"I hope you understand what I'm aiming at, because it's different from the way we've been handling this in the past, and I don't want you to be surprised if you do get restricted. If you stop fighting, we can enjoy each other a lot more—and even like each other more. That's really important to me, and I hope it is to you, too."

After this brief lecture, keep yourself in control and carry out any punishment if (or when) they are at each other's throats again. The success of your approach depends on two things: (1) saying it in a direct, no-nonsense, but calm manner; and (2) consistently carrying out what you say you'll do. (You may want to let them know what the restrictions will be in advance, so they are motivated to avoid the loss.) Both actions on your part require thinking realistic preferences instead of awfulizing, shoulding, or rationalizing. Give it a good try! They may test you—so hang in there. Be consistent and carry out the consequences. Don't keep threatening—just do it!

Young Sex

Your 15-year-old daughter begins her first romantic relationship with a fellow from school whose friends call him a stud. He is a very popular guy, and she is really thrilled that he's interested in her. She talks about him constantly to her girlfriends, and it all seems very cute. Lately, however, she's been asking *you* direct questions about what boys like most about girls, and also why they drop them. You come home early one night from a bad movie and find her and her guy sexually entwined on the couch, barely clothed.

Step 1: How am I inappropriately feeling and acting?

Extremely angry, shocked, embarrassed, and upset. Stare in amazement, shuffle around, step into the next room and yell loudly to my daughter, "Get him out of here before I kill him, and get up to your room right now!" Then storm into her room and read her the riot act, *or* cry profusely and let her know how she has destroyed me. (Some parents might make believe they didn't see anything, and deny the whole incident). In this example, we'll pursue the parent who blows up and loses it.)

Step 2: What am I irrationally thinking to make myself excessively anxious, angry, depressed, guilty, or behave inappropriately?

a: What am I thinking about myself?

"I've failed as a parent! I *should* have seen this coming, and *ought* to have done something to prevent this. I'm ashamed, I'm so embarrassed! What an idiot I am!"

b: What am I thinking about the others?

"How could she do this to us? She could be pregnant already! She's destroying her life, and ours along with it. It's that boy's fault, he made her do this. That ...!"

c: What am I thinking about the situation?

"Oh, this is awful! She'll never see him again; I'll see to that! We've got to put a stop to this immediately, if it's not already too late. If he even goes near her again, I'll kill him!"

Step 3: How can I challenge my irrational thinking?

"She has obviously been sexually involved with him, although I don't know to what extent. She might even be pregnant. That would be a very serious situation—but even that is not awful, terrible, and horrible unless *I* make it. Are they really rotten people for having done this? No. Will getting overly upset, yelling, and screaming help now, or reverse what's already happened? No. Will damning myself, or threatening her, lead to any good solutions? No, and maybe even to the opposite."

Step 4: What realistic preferences can I substitute for my irrational thinking?

"I'd have liked my daughter to use good judgment here, but it's not *awful* and she's not a *louse* because she didn't. I am seriously concerned about this, and I'm committed to letting her know how strongly I feel about her behavior, but I don't have to yell and scream at her to convey how upset I am. I want to talk with her about why she did this, and what our expectations are, but I don't need to make her feel guilty or berate her. I'd have liked her boyfriend to be more responsible, too, but he wasn't, and I will deal with him and his parents also without blowing up. I'm disappointed, highly displeased, and worried—but it's not the end of the world, and I can stop myself from overreacting."

This set of thoughts enables you as a parent to do several things: (a) express your legitimate feelings (sadness/frustration/disapproval/anxiety) in an appropriate manner without blowing up; (b) discuss with her why she did this; (c) state your expectations for the future; and (d) restrict her as you think fits (assuming she in fact violated a parental standard).

The primary emphasis would be on dealing with the future, coming to agreement on acceptable attitudes and behavior, and teaching your daughter how to deal with sexual pressures. But there also may be a legitimate place for restriction. On such critical issues as sexual behavior, it's important to get agreement, understanding, and cooperation because such activity is very difficult to prevent as well as to control. But her behavior was also a violation of parental rules that may warrant some penalty.

You might say to her (after you've thought it through and survived the shock), "I'm really stunned and upset that you decided to be sexually involved with John. I want to talk with you about why you did this, and what's at stake for you. I think you used very poor judgment, and you clearly broke the rules here."

Although it will likely be a difficult conversation for her, hopefully she will share some of her reasons and feelings with you. Although you would like her to open up and be honest, you also may want to convey that you think she made a serious mistake, and may be penalized for it. It's not easy to be a concerned parent, counselor, *and* disciplinarian on the same issue. The best you can do is keep the three as separate as possible in your talk with her. It's obviously not easy either to remain firm and serious without becoming enraged by a situation like this. That's why it's important to think realistic preferences and not to awfulize, should, or rationalize. You *can* convey the seriousness of such a situation *without* exploding.

For the parent who might avoid this situation altogether and deny it happened, rationalization would be the likely type of thinking: "What can I do? I can't watch her every minute! She has a mind of her own. I just hope they were careful. I guess times have changed. Kids are so different today. I can't say anything to her; I'd be so embarrassed, I'd die! Maybe just having walked in on them will be enough to get the message across. I'm just not any good at these sort of things." These kinds of rationalizations are based upon screwball feelings of fear of rejection and of failure, and the irrational belief, "It's easier to avoid difficult situations than to face and try to solve them."

Step 3: How can I challenge my irrational thinking?

"It *is* difficult to deal with these kinds of situations, but why is it *too* difficult? I can't watch her every minute, but why can't I at least tell her how I feel, and discuss this matter with her? Is it really easier, in the long run, to avoid facing things? Will I solve anything by not talking to both of them?"

Step 4: What realistic preferences could I substitute for my irrational thinking (that would help me to deal with this directly)?

"I'd like to convince myself that it's OK to avoid this incident, but it's not. I *am* responsible as a parent, and I'd better face my responsibility. It's not embarrassing unless I *make* it so. Although times have changed, and now I can't *make* my daughter follow my rules, I still want her to understand the importance of sexuality—to be more responsible, to know my expectations clearly, and to realize that there are consequences and penalties. I would like her to agree with me—but whether she does or not, I am committed to discussing this with her, and working toward a solution." With this type of thinking, the rationalizer will be more likely to speak up and take parental responsibility.

The primary focus of this book is on directing and controlling how we respond *inside* (what we think), in order to keep people from pushing our buttons. A sequel to this book will focus even more on *what to say to* the button-pushers. We can of course give a few examples in *these* chapters of what to say, but they are not at all the only ways to handle the situations. We are convinced, though, that if you can direct and control your awfulizing, shoulding, and rationalizing, and not let the other person get to you, you have a much better chance of handling the situation effectively.

Sometimes, as a parent, you can upset yourself with your son or daughter's *attitude*, as opposed to a specific behavior. Maybe she is becoming incredibly negative about school, or is becoming insensitive, irresponsible, or selfish. Let's say she is being disrespectful to *you*.

You *should* on her by thinking: "Just who does she think she is? I bend over backwards to make her life easier, and this is the way I get thanked! She should be thankful we let her do *anything*, with *her* lousy attitude! If she thinks she can walk around here treating me like dirt, she's got another think coming. I'll show her, that brat!"

You could add a dose of awfulizing by thinking to yourself: "What if this gets worse, and I can't control her at all? What if she really hates me? What if she's hanging around with bad kids who are putting these nasty attitudes in her head? That would be horrible! What if she doesn't change? Oh, Lord!" These thoughts could easily get you overly upset.

Or, you could rationalize: "Maybe she's just going through a phase. She's been under a lot of strain lately. I don't need to be a mean parent all the time; maybe if I ignore it she'll stop. She's really a good kid—I just have to give her some room. There's really nothing I can do, anyway. I suppose she has to express her feelings somehow, no matter what I and others think."

If you are awfulizing and shoulding, you will likely get into a nasty, emotionally agitated fight with your daughter. If you rationalize, you will likely avoid the situation and be miserable—but her behavior will persist.

Couldn't you, however, think in terms of realistic preferences?: "I *want* my daughter to speak respectfully to me. I'd *like* her to care enough to be decent and sensitive. If she isn't, it's not awful, terrible, and horrible. I'm disappointed in her behavior. I'm seriously concerned, and I'm committed to taking action and getting her to change—but I *do not* have to make myself excessively upset."

If you think in this manner, you will likely confront your daughter in a firm, direct, honest (and appropriate) manner. Even if she continues to be obnoxious or defensive, *you* won't lose your cool unless you start awfulizing or shoulding on her. Keep thinking in terms of preferences: "I *want* her to treat me with respect, but if she doesn't, I don't have to make myself overly upset. I can't thoroughly control her, but I can control how I react to her. *She* doesn't make me upset, *I* do—and I can *not* upset myself, too."

You are then free to confront her directly, without contributing to the fight: "Honey, I want to talk with you about your attitude toward me, and how you've been acting. I don't want to argue with you; I want to *discuss* it with you. This is important." If she gets defensive, sarcastic, or condescending, confront that immediately—but not with hostility: "Right now I want to talk with you, and you're acting bored [or defensive]. We can do this two ways: One is to discuss it without any nasty dramatics, and the other is to have a fight. If we fight, you wind up getting punished—and we'll both be miserable. I'd rather discuss this with you. Will you do that?"

The ball is now in her court—and if she doesn't choose to discuss, you'd better be ready to punish her *with no shouting on your part*. Also, increase the penalties or restrictions if she persists in being rude or disrespectful. *How* you tell her this will be critical. If you present the options with a tone of voice that sounds like a dare ("OK, sister—you have two choices...") or as if you are talking down to her ("You're acting like a child right now!"), you are inviting defensiveness. Again, if you are clear in your mind that you do *not* have to *win* the fight, but rather that you want to keep your cool and take appropriate actions, you will not let her push your buttons. As we have said before, though, handling this kind of situation takes lots of practice (and we're sure you'll have lots of chances). Over and over remind yourself of your preferences and of your commitment not to lose control by awfulizing or shoulding.

So many people say, "But, it's not that easy when it's your own flesh and blood!" Of course it's not *easy!* And because it's your own flesh and blood, it's even more important for you to work hard at maintaining self-control. You owe it to yourself and to the kids to keep a grip on yourself, and to show them how to as well. It *is* harder—and it's worth it.

Or is it *too* hard? It's easy to rationalize and say, "It sounds great, but—it's *too* hard," or "That's just not the way it is in real life," or "I just can't do it." If you *believe* that you can't do it, you *won't*. It is easier to avoid difficult tasks than to face them. It is easier to just make yourself upset, let 'em have it, and storm away. But that does little good in the long run. Changing your thinking requires systematic, diligent effort. But that *works*—and the long-term payoffs invariably are great for both you and your whole family.

The Loose Cannon

Your son is responsible for cleaning his room, feeding and caring for his dog and fish, and keeping the car you just got him for his 16th birthday in good working order. You cannot get the door to his room open, it's so cluttered in there—and the air around his door has a brownish color to it, like smog. The dog is never fed, and needs a bath. All the fish are gradually going belly-up. And the car has a broken taillight (backed into a fence), a "lost" tailpipe, and 450 pieces of trash on the back seat—including some that seem to be reproducing themselves.

Step 1: How am I inappropriately feeling and acting?

Extremely angry and resentful because I often clean up after him. Yell at him: "You act like you live in a pigsty! You think the whole world is your garbage can! Don't you have *any* sense of responsibility? I *knew* you wouldn't take care of your pets like you swore you would! I *knew* I'd wind up with all the work! Well, I'm tired of being the maid around here. No more, mister!"

Step 2: What am I irrationally thinking to make myself excessively anxious, angry, depressed, guilty, or behave inappropriately?

a: What am I thinking about myself?

"I'm a jerk for being his maid. I *should* have known he wouldn't take care of his pets. I've *got to* get him to shape up!"

b: What am I thinking about the others?

"He's so lazy he doesn't do *anything!* He just doesn't care [and he *should*]! He just glides through the world at everybody else's expense, that lazy...!" He doesn't have any respect for anybody or anything [and he *ought* to!]."

    c: What am I thinking about the situation?

    "I can't live like this anymore. He's driving me crazy!"

Step 3: How can I challenge my irrational thinking?

    "Although his behavior and attitude *are* frustrating, *must* I make myself crazy? Does he *have to* care and be responsible, or else I'm a jerk and he's a creep?"

Step 4: What realistic preferences can I substitute for my irrational thinking?

    "I *want* him to be more responsible and he isn't, but obviously he doesn't *have* to be, or else I can't stand it. I am disappointed in him, and seriously concerned about his attitude and his behavior—but I *can* stand it. I am also committed to dealing with him directly and firmly, but without overreacting. I'd *like* him to appreciate the importance of being responsible and so not taking advantage of others. If he does, that would be wonderful, but if he does not, I will continue to show him that there are consequences to being irresponsible."

Thinking realistic preferences will make it possible for you to confront your son with specific examples of his irresponsibility, stating what your reasonable expectations are and what the consequences will be if he doesn't deliver. For example: "When you don't feed Buster, or pick up the dirty clothes and old food in your room, then either it doesn't get done at all, or someone else—like *me*—does it for you, and that's really frustrating. I'd like you to take that seriously and correct it on your own, because you *know* what's right. If you keep on being irresponsible, I'm going to penalize you. For example, if your car is a mess, you can't drive it. If your room is a mess, you are grounded. If Buster isn't fed, you don't get to do something you would enjoy doing [be specific]. I'd much rather see you just take the responsibility and do these few things—and the problem's solved. But if you don't take things seriously, there will be real consequences. Let's see if we can solve this without getting to that point. Is that O,K. with you?"

If your son gives excuses, or is defensive or nasty, confront him with his behavior: "If I criticize you for not being responsible, and you give me excuses or get nasty, I assume that you are not willing to shape up, and that you think it's OK to talk to me like that. It's *not*. I expect you to talk with me about this in an honest and respectful manner. If you don't, you'll be penalized [be specific] for that as well." If he keeps being obnoxious, penalize him just as you said you would. If not, praise him for knocking it off and showing some real maturity.

Me, Me, Me!

One of your children is very protective of *her* room, *her* clothes, *her* things (such as a phone or stereo or bike). She refuses to lend anything to her brothers or sisters, but is always borrowing things from them. When asked to help around the house, she often complains, "That's not mine. Why should *I* have to clean it up?" Yet she's very willing to have others clean up for her.

Step 1: How am I inappropriately feeling and acting?

Disgusted, sick and tired of her selfish attitude, furious. Tell her what a self-centered snot she's become; lecture her on what it was like for me as a kid; smack her.

Step 2: What am I thinking to make myself excessively anxious, angry, depressed, or behave inappropriately?

a: What am I thinking about myself?

"I hate it when she's so selfish! How could I have raised such a mean kid? Is she just imitating *me?*"

b: What am I thinking about the others?

"She's just become a brat. All she does is whine and manipulate. All she ever thinks of is herself. Everything's 'my' this and 'my' that. I've raised a greedy, grabby monster!"

c: What am I thinking about the situation?

"She's driving me crazy! It's a constant battle. It feels hopeless."

Step 3: How can I challenge my irrational thinking?

"She *is* acting selfishly, but where is it written that she *must not* be? It is disruptive to the family, but why can't I bear it?

Will it be awful, terrible, and horrible unless I make it so? Will my getting upset and yelling at her make it any better?"

Step 4: What realistic preferences can I substitute for my irrational thoughts?

"I'd *like her* to be more balanced in her giving and taking, but there's no reason that she *has* to be. I want her to help other family members more, but I can handle it and lead a happy life if she doesn't. I expect her to change her attitude and be more willing to share, but it isn't the end of the world if she doesn't. I am *seriously concerned* about her attitude and her behavior, and will keep talking with her without blowing up—although in some cases, I will punish her for acting inappropriately."

Thinking realistic preferences would help you to be able to confront her distasteful selfishness without putting her down with (for example) "Listen, young lady—just who do you think you are? You're not the only person in this family! You'd better knock off this gimme, gimme, gimme stuff, and fast, or you'll be sorry!" You might instead confront her with "You borrow, but don't share—and refuse to help when it's not strictly your mess. You aren't doing your part to contribute to this family, and I get the impression that you think that only what *you* want counts. I'm really concerned about that, and I don't like it."

You might get a defensive excuse back, or sulking, and that can be confronted also: "If I talk with you about this and you give me a bunch of excuses, you don't seem to be willing to take responsibility for your behavior." If, after asking her to cooperate more, you still don't get a commitment, you can state your expectations ("I expect you to do your part in helping voluntarily, and to share more") and the potential consequences ("I'd like you to agree with what I'm saying, and that we will work on this together. But if you fight it, you will be penalized when you act too selfishly.")

As with so many other of these examples, there may be important reasons *why* your children are showing signs that their problematical behavior (attention-seeking, jealousy, insecurity) is in need not only of understanding but also of adjusting—pretty darn quick. But if you don't also deal with your *own* upsetness and frustration, you will be of little help to either them or the situation. We have seen many parents who "overpsychologize" their children's behavior to the point where they spend all their time trying to understand the deep, underlying causes thereof, but do little about the behavior itself or their reactions to it.

Understanding and sensitivity can be clearly important here. For example, over several days my (A.L.'s) eight-year-old daughter was acting increasingly sulky, negative, and withdrawn. We became more and more aware of this as one particular day went on. That night, while we were talking about a movie we were all watching, she broke down in tears. After a fair amount of sobbing, she couldn't really say what was troubling her, but Mom said, "Do you want some hugs?" (That's a phrase we had been using with our two-year-old a lot lately.) She nodded yes, and began sobbing heavily again. She finally told us that she had felt gradually left out as her younger sister had gotten a lot more attention. In fact, she was a great "big sister," but we were not realizing that she was upsetting herself about getting less attention.

If we had confronted only her sulking and negativity, we would have missed something important. But there were *two* issues here! One, for us to give her more love, attention, and reassurance. Two, to show her *how* to let us know when she was feeling left out, without sulking and whining. These both are important issues—and the latter can be as important as the former. We *all* make mistakes with each other. *How* we deal with those situations when we are the *recipient* will determine how well we resolve them.

These have been just a few examples of parenting situations to get you thinking of your own real circumstances, and how to apply the four steps to them. It will take practice for you to get really good at using the steps, but at least some success can come quickly. Remember to persevere! Keep thinking realistic preferences and attacking your awfulizing, shoulding, and rationalizing. In the following Exercises section you'll find some more situations you might encounter, and examples of the four different types of thinking you *could* engage in. See how different your behavior could be when your thinking changes!

EXERCISES

Exercise 8A: Changing Your Emotional and Behavioral Overreactions and Your Irrational Thinking in Situations Involving Parenting Problems and Difficulties With Your Parents

This exercise will give you practice in discovering and changing your emotional and behavioral overreactions and your irrational thinking in situations involving parenting problems or difficulties with your own parents. First, think of specific pertinent situations in which you tend to overreact, and then identify what you are irrationally thinking at that time.

Sample Practice Sheet for Exercise 8A: Discovering Your Emotional and Behavioral Overreactions and Your Irrational Thinking in Situations Involving Parenting Problems and Difficulties With Your Parents

Specific Situation	Your Emotional and Behavioral Overreactions	Your Irrational Thinking At That Time
My children disobey me and get into serious trouble.	Rage; shame and guilt. Setting even more rigid rules for the children.	How could they do that to me? Those rotten kids! I *should* have been clearer and given them better rules to follow. Obviously, I'm a rotten parent!
My children's teachers blame me for not supervising the kids' homework properly.	Anxiety; anger at children's teachers.	I *shouldn't* have been careless about supervising their homework. Their teachers must think that I am a weakling. Those damned kids lied to me about their homework, and took advantage of me. They should be severely punished!
My parents are tyrannical and don't give me the respect and freedom that other children have.	Hostility, rebelliousness.	I demand that my parents give me more respect and real freedom! I'll fix them!

Your Practice Sheet for Exercise 8A: Discovering Your Emotional and
Behavioral Overreactions and Your Irrational Thinking in Situations
Involving Parenting Problems and Difficulties With Your Parents

Specific Situation	Your Emotional and Behavioral Overreactions	Your Irrational Thinking At That Time

Sample Practice Sheet for Exercise 8B: Changing Your Irrational Thinking in Situations Involving Parenting Problems and Difficulties with Your Parents

Irrational Beliefs	Challenging and Disputing My Irrational Beliefs
How could they do that to me? Those rotten kids! I *should* have been clearer and given them better rules to follow. Obviously, I'm a rotten parent!	They're just kids. They *behaved* rottenly, but they are not totally *rotten kids*. I know I should have given them clearer and better rules, but I'll learn from my errors and do better from now on. I know this one problem doesn't make me a really bad parent.
I shouldn't have been careless about supervising their homework. Their teachers must think that I am a weakling. Those damned kids lied to me about their homework, and took advantage of me. They should be severely punished!	It is too bad that I was somewhat careless about supervising them, but I don't *have to be* a great parent all of the time. If their teachers think I'm a weakling, that is their problem. It's not the end of the world. My kids aren't perfect, but they are not rotten kids and don't deserve severe punishment in this case.
I demand that my parents give me more respect and real freedom! I'll fix them!	It would be great if my parents respected me and gave me real freedom. But they obviously don't *have to* do so. Rebellion against them will only get me into more trouble and encourage them to be even stricter. My parents are overly strict, but nobody's perfect.

Your Practice Sheet for Exercise 8B: Changing Your Irrational
Thinking in Situations Involving Parenting Problems and Difficulties
with Your Parents

Irrational Beliefs	Challenging and Disputing My Irrational Beliefs

Chapter 9

A Plethora
of Button-Pushers

We love that word "plethora"—it so accurately describes the diversity of button-pushers discussed here. The past several chapters have focused on three major aspects of the lives of many of us: the job, spousal relationships, and parenting. Yet there are dozens of lifestyles and contexts wherein we encounter other button-pushers. For instance, not everyone marries and has a family. In fact, soon there will be more single adult persons than married couples, for the first time in the history of this country. Too, many people permanently choose a single lifestyle, while others marry only later in life. And of course divorce is an increasingly common event—even as lifespans increase to the point where we often can outlive our spouse (or ex-spouse).

Being single presents a whole different set of situations that can push buttons: balancing work, chores, and tasks while dating, making friends, and otherwise trying to have a social life. And there is *still* the apparently deathless suspicion that something is wrong with you if you choose to be "single for too long."[15] Meanwhile, you may have

[15]In spite of the actual number of single persons, it takes years and years for traditional societal expectations and biases to change and catch up to reality. During these transitions, many people get caught in the middle, between what they would choose (to be single) and what society stills expects (marriage). How they *think* about that dilemma will determine how they feel, and even what they choose to do.

to deal with rejections, failures, unfair treatment, loneliness, hassles with relatives and parents, and just finding time to get everything done. Obviously there are lots of positive experiences, too—but the negatives certainly do occur. How we think about each incident is what will largely determine the overall quality of our lives.

Regardless of the lifestyle we have, we all run into tons of day-to-day situations that we can let push our buttons. We can make ourselves tremendously upset over the many decisions we have to make: buying a house, changing jobs or careers, choosing to retire, selecting investments. We can awfulize, should, and rationalize over every one of these life decisions, and/or the people we have to deal with when making them. And very often our own "nutty" thinking plays a major role in the decisions that ultimately affect our entire lives.

We also have to deal with ongoing daily hassles. To cite just a few familiar ones: an obnoxious waiter who could ruin your dinner; the nosy or gossipy neighbor who intrudes on your world; the parents who try to make you feel guilty for not visiting more, or who constantly criticize you; the cleaners who lost your new suit on the day of the big event; the airline ticket agent who was rude; the plumber who takes three weeks to fix the leak, then charges an exorbitant rate; the furniture store that promises to deliver your new sofa on Friday morning, but you wait all day with no show; the creditor who has promised "The check's in the mail" for two weeks; the car that breaks down right after you paid $500 to get it fixed; and the unexpected bills that always manage to pop up just when things are looking better. The divorced person may additionally have to deal over and over with the ex-spouse, the children (if any), financial bickering, future uncertainties, and a changed lifestyle.

As you now know, it's really how *you* think about these "things" that determine how upset you make yourself. You run into so many situations, though, in the course of a week that you literally have dozens (and sometimes hundreds) of opportunities to work on not letting them get to you. Here is just a representative sample to give you an opportunity to see how you can use the four steps of anti-button-pushing. See which ones might push *your* buttons.

"Hey, Waiter—a Minute!"

You are at a fine restaurant for a special event (birthday, anniversary, celebrating promotion). Everything else is wonderful (lovely atmosphere, great company, excellent food), but the waiter is increasingly arrogant and incompetent. He is very, very slow at everything, ignores your table for long periods, acts annoyed at your questions about the menu, makes several mistakes with your order, and is generally pompous and rude.

Step 1: How am I inappropriately feeling and acting if I let him push my buttons?

Very angry and upset, distracted from the fun, grumbling.

Step 2: What am I irrationally thinking to make myself excessively anxious, angry, depressed, guilty, or behave inappropriately?

a: What am I thinking about myself?

"I don't have to stand for this! I *ought to* stand up to this jerk. What makes him think he can treat me this way? I'm having a lousy time, and it's my fault for not telling him off!"

b: What am I thinking to myself about the others?

"He should be fired! He's ruining the whole dinner. He's a real jerk. Everybody's getting upset, I've *got to* do something."

c: What am I thinking about the situation?

"The whole evening's ruined. How can I celebrate with this fool disrupting everything? I *can't stand it* when I get rotten service!"

Step 3: How can I challenge my irrational thinking?

"The waiter *is* doing a poor job, but can he really ruin the whole evening unless I let him? Do I *have to* dwell on this and make myself overly upset and angry?"

Step 4: What realistic preferences can I substitute for my irrational thinking?

"I'd like the service to be better, but it's not. That's not awful, but it *is* frustrating. I can confront the waiter or speak to the manager, but I do not have to get myself overly upset in the process. Why *must* he act differently? *I* decide how much or how little I let this waiter affect my mood and the evening. *I* am committed to doing something about it *and* to enjoying myself."

If, however, you let this person really get to you by awfulizing and shoulding, you might wind up berating him loudly and disrupting the party (the direct route) or saying nothing and leaving no tip (which nonactions he perhaps deserves). If you are thinking rationalizations ("Maybe he's just busy or is having a bad day" or "He could be new on the job"), you might just avoid the whole problem as best you can. But if you are thinking realistic preferences, you would likely confront the waiter privately in a direct, albeit respectful, manner about this: "When you ignore our table for long periods and sound annoyed about our questions regarding the menu, we are not receiving very good service and it seems you are indifferent about it." Depending on how he responds (and whether he shapes up fast), you might also go to the manager and register the same complaint—again in a direct but appropriate manner. If you wait until you are fed up, and blow up at either of them, they may think it's you who are out of line, and ignore you. If the service was poor for most of the meal, you would still leave a minimal tip—if any.

Being Single

You have been a bachelor for some time, but have never been very good at this "first encounter" stuff. You are at a cocktail party and see someone across the room who looks attractive and interesting.

Step 1: How am I inappropriately feeling and acting if I let this push my buttons?

Extremely anxious, sweating, avoiding any contact.

Step 2: What am I irrationally thinking to make myself excessively anxious, angry, depressed, guilty, or behave inappropriately?

a: What am I thinking about myself?

"What if I blow it again? What if I get all tongue-tied and look like a fool? I'd be so embarrassed! I'm just not any good at this stuff [and I *should* be]."

b: What am I thinking about the others?

"What if she's with someone? What if she thinks I'm a jerk? What if she's got someone else in mind here?"

c: What am I thinking about the situation?

"This 'pickup' stuff is so superficial! How can you possibly really get to know anyone here? It's all so phony! I hate it! Maybe I'll just meet someone at work, or through friends. I just can't do this!"

Step 3: How can I challenge my irrational thinking?

"Do I really *have to* be good at this to do it, anyway? Do I *have to* have her like me? Am I really a failure if this person fails to be interested in me? Could I handle it if she is with someone, or is interested in someone else and not me? Even if cocktail parties *can* be superficial, does that mean I *shouldn't* introduce myself?"

Step 4: What realistic preferences can I substitute for my irrational thinking?

"I'd *like* to introduce myself and have her show interest in me. I'd *like* to get to know her and to talk with her a bit. If she does, that would be very nice. If she doesn't, that's unfortunate. I'd regret it, but it is not something I need to avoid. Even though cocktail parties *can* be superficial, that doesn't mean *I* have to be, nor is that a justification for avoiding meeting her. Rejection is not devastating— and that's the *worst* thing that could happen."

By challenging the awfulizing about possibly being rejected, *and* the rationalizing to justify avoiding her, you are better able to approach her. You didn't try to convince yourself that you would do fine, or that you were great, with positive affirmations. You challenged the heart of the issue: Is rejection really as bad as we sometimes tell ourselves, and can we think about it more realistically? Then, whether you were successful or not, whether you liked the way you approached her or not, whether she liked you or not, doesn't matter that much. You did it: You challenged the fears of rejection and failure! (P.S.: If you don't go ahead and approach her, don't should on yourself! Keep working on challenging your awfulizing, and don't give up!)

Sorry—It's the *Rules!*

You just bought a used boat and trailer, and you can't wait to get them registered so you can take the boat out for a spin. You go to the Department of Motor Vehicles. It's about a half-hour drive, and when you get there, a line is extending all the way out the door and around the side of the building. You make a wish (optimist that you are) that that's not your line—but it is. You find out that the computers are down and that the wait is at least four hours. You come back several days later, and the line is down to a "normal" one-hour wait, so you stay. Finally, it's your turn! You show the clerk the pink slips for the boat and trailer; she starts typing up the papers; she tells you how much the sales tax and registration fees will be (the total is enough to blow your stack); and then she makes a funny face and says, "Uh-oh." Your heart starts beating a little faster.

There's a pregnant pause while the clerk stares at your pink slips (she seems to be savoring the moment). You blurt out, "Is there anything wrong?" She looks up with a steely smile and says, "I'm afraid so, sir. On your boat pink slip it says 'John *or* Mary Snodgrass' as the seller, which only requires the signature of one of them. On your trailer it says 'John/Mary Snodgrass.' The DMV policy is to interpret slashes as 'and,' not '*or*.' You only have John Snodgrass's signature, sir. I cannot complete this application, and you may not operate this trailer until said application is properly transferred with both persons' signatures." She hands your paperwork back and shouts "Next!" John and Mary have moved to someplace in Montana, and you don't know where.

Step 1: How are you inappropriately feeling and acting?

Furious, angry, bummed out, helpless, depressed. Yell, scream, throw a tantrum (act like Steve Martin in *Planes, Trains, and Automobiles* when the car-rental bus left him in the faraway lot with no car there); or sink to the floor and crawl out babbling to yourself.

Step 2: What am I thinking to make myself excessively anxious, angry, depressed, guilty, or act inappropriately?

a: What am I thinking about myself?

"I can't stand this bureaucratic bull! This is insane! All I want to do is register my boat and trailer and go have some fun. I don't deserve this. I should have checked more carefully and made *both* of them sign. What a dope I am for not doing that!"

b: What am I thinking about the others?

"That bitch! She could overlook this if she wanted. No one would notice. Damn her. She even looks like she's enjoying it. I hope she chokes!"

c: What am I thinking about the situation?

"Bureaucracy! I *hate* bureaucracy! Picky, picky, picky! They're not here to help, they're here to torment us. And *we* pay their salaries! It's just not fair! (as it should be)."

Step 3: How can I challenge my irrational thinking?

"I'll never *like* this bureaucratic bull, but why can't I *stand* it? I did get his signature, but how could I have known that I needed his wife's as well? What makes that clerk a total bitch for bureaucratically sticking to the rules? It's very inconvenient, but what makes it *awful?* Does the world always have to be fair?"

Step 4: How can I substitute realistic preferences for my irrational thinking?

"I'd like this process to have gone smoothly, but it hasn't. That's very frustrating; it's bad enough that I can't use the boat right away, and have to start over again. But I don't *have to* make myself needlessly angry and depressed as well. It would have been better had I made sure I got both signatures, but there's no reason I *absolutely should* have done so. Even if it isn't fair, it doesn't *have to be* fair. I can write and complain, or I can request a quicker solution when I return [go to front of line] or mail it in. Whatever the policies are, I can handle it without upsetting myself."

P.S.: This was a real situation and, in fact, because I (A.L.) did not rile myself up, the clerk gave me several suggestions as to how I could complete the registration right away without starting all over again. As I was dealing with my situation, the person at the counter next to me was having a problem, too, and decided to be very rude and verbally belligerent with the clerk—who proceeded to go strictly "by the book" and get him good. It doesn't always turn out better just because you exercise self-control, but sometimes it helps. Some people believe that intimidation and blowing up "works," too. Certainly it is true that the wheel that squeaks the loudest gets the grease. But wheels are not people—and if that's your philosophy, you may win a few rounds but you will often lose the contest. "They" can often get you back! Remember, you can still be firmly assertive and stand up for your rights without overreacting and losing your cool.

If You Really Loved Me, You'd...

Your mother lives nearby, and ever since you've moved out of the house she has pressured you to visit every day. You care for her a great deal, but she doesn't seek out friends her own age, and tries to manipulate you into being her constant companion. She expects you to come by and call every day, or else she is depressed and miserable.

Step 1: How am I inappropriately feeling and acting?

  Guilty, down on myself, resentful, avoiding her, giving lame excuses and/or giving in a lot more than I'd like.

Step 2: What am I thinking to make myself excessively anxious, angry, depressed, or guilty, or behave inappropriately?

  a: What am I thinking about myself?

  "I must really be an ingrate. Look at all she's done for me. The least I could do is spend more time with her. But I've got to live my own life, too. Yeah, but what if she had said that when I needed *her?* She's all alone; she needs me. I owe her. [What a louse I am for not being the caring child I *should* be!]"

  b: What am I thinking about the others?

  "She's so manipulative [and she shouldn't be!]. She plays helpless just to make me feel bad, and I do. She's incredibly sneaky, and I always give in. Why can't she make friends with people her own age? But she *is* alone, and seems so lonely. She *is* my mother."

  c: What are you thinking about the situation?

  "I just hate saying no to her. I can't win, no matter what I do. How can I please everybody, including me? I just hate this whole thing. It's not fair [and it *should* be!]."

Step 3: How can I challenge and dispute my irrational thinking?

  "She does try to make me feel guilty. *Must* I get overly upset about that? Does not wanting to spend as much time with her as she wants make me a rotten person? Does her manipulation make *her* rotten? Even if it's unfair that I have a demanding mother, must the world always be fair to me?"

Step 4: What realistic preferences can I substitute for my irrational thinking?

"I'd *prefer* that my mom be less manipulative, but I don't *need* her to be, and I don't have to should on her for it. I'd *like* her to spend *some* time with me *and* find others to enjoy as well. I'd like to be close with her but not see her every day, nor be her sole companion. If she thinks that makes me a neglectful child, I can handle that. I am concerned that she is not attempting to meet others, and it's frustrating when she tries to manipulate me—but she's not a rotten person, nor am I a weakling if I sometimes give in. I am committed to talking with her about what I want and do not want to do. I can do this without making myself upset or letting her push my buttons. I can let her know that I care very much, and exactly what kind of time commitment I can and will make."

Thinking realistic preferences will enable you to say to your mother something like, "Mom, I love you very much, and I want to see you, but I am not willing to visit every day or be your only companion." You might also let her know that it's frustrating when she tries to make you feel guilty for not being there every day, and that you'd like her to stop acting that way. You can do all this while keeping calm and assuring her of your love.

If you awfulize or should on her in your head, you will likely be harsher and more exasperated, and convey the wrong message. If you rationalize or should on yourself, you might let her manipulate you into spending more time than is good for you or her. Moreover, your resentment will come out eventually.

Every person and every relationship is different as to how much time is "appropriate" to spend. Differences will often exist as to what is desirable or acceptable. These differences can be resolved through discussion and compromise, but not if a lot of shoulding ("You should...") and awfulizing ("It's awful when she...") is going on. It can be difficult to discuss these things with people you care about, but when you are successful it can bring you much closer together.

What, Me Worry?

You are doing some remodeling of your home. You engage a contractor to put in sliding, tinted-glass doors in the bedroom. Six weeks later (he said they would be there in three) he shows up with the doors and they are clear, not tinted. He blames the manufacturer and takes no responsibility for checking the delivery. Three more weeks pass and he shows up with the tinted windows. Hooray! He installs them and announces proudly that the job is completed. You look at the windows and there are large, oily streaks—seemingly baked into the glass—that totally distort the view. He says, "Gee, I didn't notice that. Maybe they'll wash out."

Step 1: How am I inappropriately feeling and acting?

Furious, totally frustrated, fed up; getting into a shouting match with him! "Didn't notice it? You'd have to be blind! Just what are you trying to pull? Do you think I'm an idiot? I'm reporting you to the Better Business Bureau. You'll hear from my lawyer. You're history, pal!" Then I'm absolutely miserable for days, ruining my own time. (Interestingly, he's probably gone on to his next incompetent job, and will be totally unfazed by his screw up!).

Step 2: What am I irrationally thinking to make myself excessively anxious, angry, depressed, guilty, or act inappropriately?

a: What am I thinking about myself?

"I can't believe it! He screwed up again. Why didn't I get rid of him the first time! What a dummy I am!"

b: What am I thinking about the others?

"What a jerk! He's held up this whole project for weeks! I've never seen such incompetence! What if he refuses to do anything and I have to pay him? I couldn't bear it!"

c: What am I thinking about the situation?

"This is intolerable! Wait 'til [husband/wife] hears about this. This could drag on and on. How did I get myself into this mess? Well, I won't take it lying down. I'll scream like a banshee!"

Step 3: How can I challenge my irrational thinking?

"Am I really a dummy for letting him act so incompetently? Why can't I bear his crummy behavior? Is the situation totally intolerable? Will making myself scream and yell do any good—or will it perhaps make things worse?"

Step 4: What realistic preferences can I substitute for my irrational thinking?

"I *want* this job done right and promptly, but my life won't end if it isn't. "I'd like him to have done it right the first two times, and he hasn't. That's frustrating, and I feel very disappointed—but I don't need to make myself miserable. It's bad, but it's not unbearable. I am committed to getting this situation resolved, and to keep from overreacting."

This situation is interesting because you have several courses of action available to you, depending on the circumstances and your judgment. None of them is patently right or wrong. What *is* critical is that you not make yourself overly upset, regardless of how you choose to handle him and the situation.

If you already made the mistake of paying up-front, you might negotiate a solution with this person for prompt correction of his screwup. You also might negotiate a reduction or discount in his charges, to be returned to you (fat chance of success, but it's worth a try!). After completion of the work, you might notify the Better Business Bureau, or any other consumer-advocate group, to at least register the complaint.

If you have not paid everything yet, you might refuse full payment until the job is done right, or refuse to have the job done at all—depending on how much you've paid already. You could also take him to small-claims court, but don't count on necessarily winning anything.

When confronting him, however, *you would keep your cool* and might say: "You have failed to install the proper doors twice, and consequently set us back several weeks on our schedule. That's been extremely disruptive, and was avoidable. I want these doors re-moved, and you will not be paid for anything." (Or: "I want this done properly within a week—whatever it takes—or I will sue you for return of my payment, plus damages.")

The key to this response (and what makes it different from the responses if you are awfulizing and shoulding) is that here you did not overreact. You are taking firm action and are very angry, but you are functional and handling it assertively. Sometimes it's tough to do in situations like this, but you *can* do it!

The Great Revenge: Undermine

You are a recently divorced woman with two children, seven and nine years old. They return from a visit with your ex-spouse and are acting strangely difficult again. You ask them what's going on, and (sure enough) your ex has been saying nasty, degrading things about you again—telling the children that you are a bad parent, that you were mean to him, that he loves them more than you do, and that he misses them so much.

Step 1: How am I inappropriately feeling and acting if I let him push my buttons?

Overly upset, furious, crabbing at the kids.

Step 2: What am I thinking to get myself excessively anxious, angry, depressed, guilty, or act inappropriately?

a: What am I thinking about myself?

"I can't stand it when he does this! How can I be an effective parent when I am constantly undermined? I feel helpless with my own children [and that's not fair]. I've *got to* do something to change their father!"

b: What am I thinking about the others?

"What if they believe their father's lies and manipulations? What if he's saying even worse things? What if he turns them against me? What if he doesn't stop? Why does he have to be such a child? That louse! I'll take him to court; I'll cut off his visitation rights; I'll put a contract out on him!"

c: What am I thinking about the situation?

"This whole thing stinks and I can't really make him stop it. Why should I still have to suffer because of that creep?"

Step 3: How can I challenge my irrational thinking?

"He *is* saying disruptive things to the children, but why can't I stand it? Does *it* drive me crazy or am *I* doing this to myself? *Must I* really change their father? Does my whole life stink just because he acts slinkily? Will making myself overly upset make his manipulation go away?"

Step 4: How can I substitute realistic preferences for my irrational thinking?

"I'd prefer that he not say negative things to the children, but he *is* saying them, and I don't *have to* stop him. I regret it, and I am seriously concerned about it, but I can handle it. I am frustrated and keenly disappointed, but I don't need to overreact. I am committed to doing everything I can to see that he stops, and I can talk calmly to the children about it. It's bad enough it's happening; I don't also have to make myself miserable about it. That may even be his intent—to make me upset. But *that* I'll stubbornly refuse to be!"

If you think realistic preferences, you might call him up and say:

"When you tell the kids I'm a bad parent and make derogatory comments about me, you are hurting the kids and using them to try to hurt me. That's very frustrating, and I'm seriously concerned about it." Maybe you'd "like" to tell him he's an incredible jerk and he'd better knock it off or he won't see them again, but then you are only escalating the problem. By confronting him directly without over-reacting, you are showing that he really *can't* upset you with his comments, and that you are willing to confront him about it functionally. On the other hand, if you awfulize or should on him, you will likely blow up and have a nasty exchange, which would only prove he can still push your buttons. If you rationalize, you will do nothing but avoid the situation, hoping he will stop or the kids will ignore him. But inside you are miserable. Thinking realistic preferences is better for *you!*

The Moment of Truth

You are a woman who has been single for some time, enjoying the freedom and diversity of that lifestyle. You are however involved with someone you really love, and could imagine marrying. You have been neither pro nor con about marriage, but suddenly he pops the question, and you must make a swift decision.

Step 1: How am I inappropriately feeling and acting if I let this push my buttons?

Extremely anxious, agitated, distant, out of sorts, irritable, confused.

Step 2: What am I irrationally thinking to make myself excessively anxious, angry, depressed, guilty, or act inappropriately?

a: What am I thinking about myself?

"I love him so much, but what if I say yes, and being married messes everything up? That would be awful! What if I say no, and he leaves when he would have been a wonderful husband and we would be terribly happy? That would *really* be terrible! What if I get bored in marriage [as I shouldn't]? What if I turn him down and I wind up alone and lonely? That would be the awfulest of all! I've *got to* make the right decision. I *can't* screw this one up!"

b: What am I thinking about the others?

"What if he changes *after* we're married? What *if I* don't *really* know him? What if he's been fooling me? What an idiot I'd be. And what a worm he'd be! What if he stops being so loving, caring, interested, and affectionate? I couldn't take it! What if he tries to turn me into a homebody and insists that I stop my career? Can I really trust him?"

c: What am I thinking about the situation?

"What if it just doesn't work out? We might have to stay miserably married forever, or I'd have to start all over again. Ugh! What if it all ruins our love? It's too complex! Things *should* be simpler! Making big decisions is awful!"

Step 3: How can I challenge my irrational thinking?

"I have been single for 12 years, and I've enjoyed it. I'd *prefer* to marry, but do I *have to?* There are many uncertainties that I can't completely answer, but why must I have certainty? Our future is not guaranteed. Do I need a guarantee to make a decision? If we marry and it doesn't work out, why couldn't I stand it? If he's fooling me, would my being fooled make me an idiot—and could I handle it?

Would it be awful, terrible, and horrible if I made the wrong decision? Do I *have* to have all the answers *now?* Does getting upset help me to make a good decision?"

Step 4: What realistic preferences can I substitute for my irrational thinking?

"I very much *want* to make a good decision here, but I don't *have* to. It's not the end of the world. It *would be better if* I think logically about each issue, and trust how I feel about him without awfulizing. What I *want* is what counts. I can think clearly about the real concerns, and sort out my feelings. Whatever I decide, if it works out well, that's wonderful—but if it doesn't, I would be very sad, though I can deal with that. I am committed to doing everything I can to make my decision a good one. Once it is made, I can do a lot to influence how it turns out."

Notice that, in this case, thinking realistic preferences doesn't point you in a particular direction. You *may* or *may not* decide to get married. The goal here is to get rid of the awfulizing and shoulding that is getting in the way of your clearly dealing with an important decision. Once we start thinking more clearly, the outcome of even wrong decisions won't be deadly! We are likely to make *better* decisions all around. Even then, it might still not work out, but we *can* handle whatever happens. Getting rid of thoughts like fear of failure and rejection, and attacking the idea that bad decisions must never be made, enables us to take risks in the first place. Then we can deal with the resulting consequences and go on with our lives.

To Be—or Not to Be

You have been working successfully in your particular career for a number of years. Lately, though, you have been considering a radical change. You suddenly get an opportunity to take it, and now it's more than just talk. You *have* to decide: Someone's made you a job offer in a totally different field.

Step 1: How am I inappropriately feeling and acting if I let this push my buttons?

Highly anxious, distracted, agitated, on edge, and irritable.

Step 2: What am I irrationally thinking to myself to make myself excessively anxious, angry, depressed, guilty, or act inappropriately?

a: What am I thinking about myself?

"What if I do make the change, and I hate it? What a dope I'd be! What if I'm not very good at it? I have obligations—responsibilities. I can't just pick up and start over! But what if I don't give it a try? Then I'll never know! I'd never forgive myself. What *should* I do? Maybe I'm just going through a midlife crisis. Maybe it'll all pass in time. What a chicken! I *should* be able to make this decision without all this agony!"

b: What am I thinking about the others?

"What if I don't like working with those people? What if my family thinks I'm crazy? Everyone *should* be on my side, but, instead they're critical. They're sabotaging me! But what if they're right?"

c: What am I thinking to myself about the situation?

"What if I make the wrong choice? What if I screw up my future? I've *got to* do this right! There are too many factors; it's too complicated. I can't just stay in a rut, but I shouldn't just go out on a limb, either. What a gruesome choice. What should I do? I can't stand this dilemma!"

Step 3: How can I challenge and dispute my irrational thinking?

"Although the consequences of my making a wrong decision are great, why do I *have to* make a correct one? I wouldn't at all *like* to make a stupid move, but if I do—I do! Neither decision is irreversible. Would it be awful, terrible, and horrible if I made a choice I didn't like? Does awfulizing, shoulding, or rationalizing help me make a better decision? This is really a dilemma. Why can't I *stand* it?"

Step 4: What realistic preferences can I substitute for my irrational thinking?

"I *want* to make the best decision I can, but I could live and be happy with even a poor one. I'd like to know in advance if a career change will work out, but I can't predict that perfectly. I want to enjoy my life and provide security for my family, but I can't guarantee this. If my family doesn't fully support me, I'll live—and they're not creeps. I am committed to thinking about this decision logically, and to considering all the factors. If I do make a decision that doesn't work out as I hoped, it is not totally irreversible. I do not have to awfulize, should on myself, or rationalize when thinking this through. Whatever decision I do make, I will support it."

Just as with other major life decisions (marriage, divorce, having children), the decision itself can often be greatly influenced by awfulizing, shoulding, and rationalizing about fear of rejection, fear of failure, low frustration tolerance, and who's to blame. The goal of thinking realistic preferences is to make decisions (whatever they may be) based upon reality, logic, preferences, and other relevant factors that you think are in your best interest. You will not only likely make better decisions, but you will feel much better while making them!

There are just too many different situations that can push your buttons to cover *in toto* in this book. We hope you have gotten a taste of how the four steps can be successfully applied to similar situations in your own day-to-day life.

EXERCISES

Exercise 9A: Discovering and Changing Your Emotional and Behavioral Overreactions and Your Irrational Thinking in Various Life Situations

This exercise will give you practice in discovering and changing your emotional and behavioral overreactions and your irrational thinking in various life situations. First, think of different day-to-day situations in which you tend to overreact, and then identify specifically what you are thinking at that time to upset yourself.

Sample Practice Sheet for Exercise 9A: Discovering Your Emotional and Behavioral Overreactions and Your Irrational Thinking in Various Life Situations

Specific Situation	Your Emotional and Behavioral Overreactions	Your Irrational Thinking at That Time
Being alone.	Feeling depressed and inadequate. Not attempting to meet new people.	I'll always be alone and never have someone who truly cares for me. I'm just not good enough to have a real relationship. I'm a loser. What's the use of trying?
Having a series of real troubles and misfortunes.	Depressed; low frustration tolerance. Giving up trying to change things.	Everything bad happens to me. I can't stand it! I'm just impossibly unlucky! What's the use?
Having to make some big decisions and being afraid you'll make some terrible mistakes.	Self-downing for being indecisive. Procrastinating on making decision.	What if I make the wrong decisions? People will really think I'm an idiot. I can't bear being indecisive, and people putting me down for this!

Your Practice Sheet for Exercise 9A: Discovering Your Emotional and Behavioral Overreactions and Your Irrational Thinking in Various Life Situations

Specific Situation	Your Emotional and Behavioral Overreactions	Your Irrational Thinking at That Time

Sample Practice Sheet for Exercise 9B: Changing Your Irrational
Thinking in Various Life Situations

Irrational Beliefs	Challenging and Disputing My Irrational Beliefs
I'll always be alone and never have someone who truly cares for me. I'm just not good enough to have a real relationship. I'm a loser. What's the use of trying?	Even though I am now alone and have been alone several times before, that does not prove that I'll never have anyone to love. I probably will have a steady, fully loving relationship if I keep trying, but I won't condemn myself for my state of loneliness. It doesn't make me a bad person. I can handle this.
Everything bad happens to me. I can't stand it! I'm just impossibly unlucky! What's the use?	Many bad things have happened to me, but obviously not everything in my life is and will be bad. Although I'm having a bad time now, I *can* stand it. Maybe I'm unlucky, but I still can make some good things happen and have some enjoyment in life.
What if I make the wrong decision? People will really think I'm an idiot. I can't bear being indecisive, and people putting me down for this!	My indecision is certainly bad, but it's hardly *terrible*; and damning myself for it will not make me more decisive. People probably won't think I am an idiot for being indecisive, but if they do, I don't have to agree with them and put myself down.

Your Practice Sheet for Exercise 9B: Changing Your Irrational
Thinking in Various Life Situations

Irrational Beliefs	Challenging and Disputing My Irrational Beliefs

Chapter 10

Go Get 'Em!

We hope the main point of this book is clear by now: *People and things don't* push our buttons. Not really. Rather, *we* push *our own* buttons—when we awfulize, should on ourselves and others, and rationalize. *We* push our buttons when we worry *too much* about what others think of us, when we worry *too much* about getting respect, when we *excessively* fear failing or making fools of ourselves, when we *overreact* if things don't turn out as we insist, when we're *not* treated fairly, and when we *blame* ourselves or others harshly. Even when others are trying to push our buttons they can only succeed if we let them!

We all have feelings about what's happening in our lives. That's natural and healthy. The goal of this book is *not* to *eliminate* feelings. The goal is to attack and reduce (if not totally eliminate) our emotional *overreactions* so that we *can* feel all kinds of feelings that are healthy and appropriate to the specific situations.

There's nothing wrong with your feeling displeased, angry, nervous, concerned, guilty, sad, or grief-stricken—or having lots of other feelings. The key is to keep those feelings at a level where you aren't making yourself utterly miserable and less effective. Don't worry: *Nobody's* perfect at it! There are very few Gandhis around. (We'll bet even Gandhi got ticked off sometimes.) *Your* goal is *improvement*. We encourage you to meet three goals for your overreactions: (1) Don't let them happen so often; (2) Make them less

193

intense when you do overreact; and (3) Don't let them last so long. We, the authors of this book, are handling things better than *we* previously did, and that's what we *keep* shooting for: *improvement*.

Your third goal, not letting your overreactions last so long, may be the most important one. How many times have you had a brief fight or nasty exchange with someone you care about, and then gone off and sulked for hours or days in a neutral corner? Maybe you even continued to snipe at each other for a while. Sometimes you can't even remember what started the stupid thing, but you surely do remember how upsetting it was, and how miserable you were during that time apart. All the while, you were indulging in some sort of awfulizing, shoulding, or rationalizing.

The keys to improvement are: (1) Be willing to admit that you are overreacting; (2) Take responsibility for changing that; and (3) Practice, over and over, the four steps for changing *from* awfulizing, shoulding, and rationalizing *to* realistic preferences. Changing your *natural* responses is hard work that requires diligent effort. Nutty thinking does not go away by itself—and we've all created or picked up some of it along the way. It's worth getting it out of our lives!

Why? Why is it worth it? For us, it's because we don't espouse the Schlitz philosophy of life. *You* know it. (No, we don't believe, "When you're out of Schlitz, you're out of beer!") If you've ever seen the old commercials, they used to say "Go for the gusto!" Now, that was the slogan—but the next line was the philosophy: "Because you only go around once!" And there are two things in life that count. First, *results!* Did you *do* the things you wanted to do, accomplish your goals, reach your destinations? Maybe they're your life goals, your career goals, your annual goals, or your list of things to do today! Did you get 'em *done?* Second—and at least as important, if not more so: Did you also, in the process of getting there, make doggone sure that you *enjoyed the trip?*

Sometimes we get so caught up in the tasks, the demands, the deadlines, the people, the hassles, the decisions that we *forget* to enjoy the trip. You "get there," but in the process you awfulize, should on yourself, and rationalize. *What* and *how* are not substitutes for each other. They *both* count. Have you ever seen that nutty bumper-sticker that says "The one who dies with the *most* toys wins?" We always look at the drivers and wonder if they ever really got to enjoy any of their toys, or were they too awfulizing and shoulding on themselves about how many toys they had (or didn't have), compared to everyone else.

How many times have you heard the cliché "It's not whether you win or lose—it's how you play the game"? The way that sentence is written is pretty stupid. Listen to it—it expects you to choose *between* the two. Is it whether you win or lose, *or* is it how you play the game? What's the best answer? In *life*, it's *both!!*

You very much *want* to be a winner at things you undertake, and you want also to enjoy the game even while paying attention to how and why you're playing it. You want to do things that you believe are meaningful and worthwhile—to the best of your ability, with pride and enthusiasm. You want to have good, healthy relationships, and to put something into them regularly. You especially want to minimize the button-pushers who get in the way of your enjoying the trip. Don't let yourself become a casualty of your own efforts in life! You only go around once. Enjoy.

Our invitation and challenge to you is clear: "Go get 'em!" And we don't mean the button-pushing people and things—we mean your own screwball thoughts and emotional overreactions. Change *them*, and you will be a winner in what *really* counts. Go get 'em!

Suggested Further Reading and Listening

A good many books, pamphlets, cassettes, and other self-help materials follow the principles of rational emotive behavior therapy (REBT) and cognitive behavior therapy (CBT), which are the basis for the techniques presented in this book. These may often be used, by themselves or together with individual or group psychotherapy, to help you and others with your emotional and behavioral problems. We recommend the following materials, most of which are obtainable from the Institute for Rational-Emotive Therapy, 45 East 65th Street, New York, NY 10021-6593, (212) 535-0822. The Institute's free catalogue, and the materials it distributes, may be ordered by phone (1-800-323-IRET), or by fax (212-249-3582). The Institute will continue to make available these and other materials, as well as to present talks, workshops, training practica, and other presentations in the area of human growth and rational living, and to list these in its regular catalogues.

Alberti, R., & Emmons, M. (1990). *Your perfect right*. San Luis Obispo, CA: Impact.

Beck, A.T. (1988). *Love is not enough*. New York: Harper.

Bernard, M.E. (1986). *Staying alive in an irrational world: Albert Ellis and rational-emotive therapy*. South Melbourne, Australia: Carlson/Macmillan; Secaucus, NJ: Carol Publishing Group.

Borcherdt, B. (1993). *You can control your feelings*. Sarasota, FL: Professional Resource Exchange.

Bourland, D.D., Jr., & Johnston, P.D. (1991). *To be or not: An E-prime anthology.* San Francisco: International Society for General Semantics.

Burns, D.D. (1980). *Feeling good: The new mood therapy.* New York: Morrow.

Corey, G., & Corey, M. (1990). *I never knew I had a choice.* Pacific Grove, CA: Brooks/Cole.

DiGiuseppe, R. (Speaker) (1990). *What do I do with my anger: Hold it in or let it out?* New York: Cassette recording. Institute for Rational-Emotive Therapy.

DiGiuseppe, R. (Speaker) (1991). *Maximizing the moment: How to have more fun and happiness in life.* New York: Cassette recording. Institute for Rational-Emotive Therapy.

Dryden, W. (1990). *Dealing with anger problems: Rational-emotive therapeutic interventions.* Sarasota, FL: Profesional Resource Exchange.

Dryden, W., & DiGiuseppe, R. (1990). *A primer on rational-emotive therapy.* Stony Stratford, England: Open University Press.

Dryden, W., & Gordon, J. (1991). *Think your way to happiness.* London: Sheldon Press.

Ellis, A. (1962). *Reason and emotion in psychotherapy.* New York: Carol Publishing Group.

Ellis, A. (1972a). *Executive leadership: The rational-emotive approach.* New York: Institute for Rational-Emotive Therapy.

Ellis, A. (1972b). *Psychotherapy and the value of a human being.* New York: Institute for Rational-Emotive Therapy.

Ellis, A. (1973). *Humanistic psychotherapy: The rational-emotive approach.* New York: McGraw-Hill.

Ellis, A. (1974). *Technique of disputing irrational beliefs (DIBS). New York: Institute for Rational-Emotive Therapy.*

Ellis, A. (1975). *How to live with a neurotic: At home and at work.* North Hollywood, CA: Wilshire Books. Original edition, 1957.

Ellis, A. (1976). RET abolishes most of the human ego. New York: Institute for Rational-Emotive Therapy.

Ellis, A. (1977). *Anger—How to live with and without it.* New York: Carol Publishing Group.

Ellis, A. (1985). *Overcoming resistance: Rational-emotive therapy with difficult clients.* New York: Springer.

Ellis, A. (1988a). *How to stubbornly refuse to make yourself miserable about anything—Yes, anything!* New York: Carol Publishing Group.

Ellis, A. (1991). Achieving self-actualization. In A. Jones & R. Crandall (Eds.). *Handbook of self-actualization.* Corte Madera, CA: Select Press.

Ellis, A. (1992). Foreword. In P. Hauck (Ed.). *Overcoming the rating game* (pp. 1–4). Louisville, KY: Westminster/John Knox.

Ellis, A., & Becker, I. (1982). *A guide to personal happiness.* North Hollywood, CA: Wilshire Books.

Ellis, A. (1994). *Reason and Emotional Psychotherapy,* revised. New York: Carol Publishing Group.

Ellis, A., & DiMattia, D. (1991). *Rational effectiveness training: A new method of facilitating management and labor relations.* New York: Institute for Rational-Emotive Therapy.

Ellis, A., & Dryden, W. (1987). *The practice of rational-emotive therapy.* New York: Springer.

Ellis, A., & Dryden, W. (1990). *The essential Albert Ellis.* New York: Springer.

Ellis, A., & Dryden, W. (1991). *A dialogue with Albert Ellis: Against dogma.* Milton Keynes, England: Open University Press.

Ellis, A., & Harper, R.A. (1975). *A new guide to rational living.* North Hollywood, CA: Wilshire Books.

Ellis, A., & Hunter, P. (1991). *Why am I always broke? How to be sane about money.* Secaucus, NJ: Lyle Stuart.

Ellis, A., & Knaus, W. (1977). *Overcoming procrastination.* New York: New American Library.

Ellis, A., McInerney, J.F., DiGuiseppe, R., & Yeager, R.J. (1988). *Rational-emotive therapy with alcoholics and substance abusers.* New York: Pergamon.

Ellis, A., Vega, G., & DiMattia, D. (1990). *Self-management: Strategies for personal success.* New York: Institute for Rational-Emotive Therapy.

Ellis, A., & Velten, E. (1962). *When AA doesn't work for you: A rational guide for quitting alcohol.* New York: Barricade Books.

Ellis, A. (Speaker) (1973a). *How to stubbornly refuse to be ashamed of anything.* New York: Cassette recording. Institute for Rational-Emotive Therapy.

Ellis, A. (Speaker) (1973b). *Twenty-one ways to stop worrying.* New York: Cassette recording. Institute for Rational-Emotive Therapy.

Ellis, A. (Speaker) (1974). *Rational living in an irrational world.* New York: Cassette recording. Institute for Rational-Emotive Therapy.

Ellis, A. (Speaker) (1975). *RET and assertiveness training.* New York: Cassette recording. Institute for Rational-Emotive Therapy.

Ellis, A. (Speaker) (1976). *Conquering low frustration tolerance.* New York: Cassette recording. Institute for Rational-Emotive Therapy.

Ellis, A. (Speaker) (1977a). *Conquering the dire need for love.* New York: Cassette recording. Institute for Rational-Emotive Therapy.

Ellis, A. (Speaker) (1977b). *A garland of rational humorous songs.* New York: Cassette recording. Institute for Rational-Emotive Therapy.

Ellis, A. (Speaker) (1978). *I'd like to stop, but... /Dealing with addiction.* New York: Cassette recording. Institute for Rational-Emotive Therapy.

Ellis, A. (Speaker) (1980). *Twenty-two ways to brighten up your love life.* New York: Cassette recording. Institute for Rational-Emotive Therapy.

Ellis, A. (Speaker) (1988). *Unconditionally accepting yourself and others.* New York: Cassette recording. Institute for Rational-Emotive Therapy.

Ellis, A. (Speaker) (1990). *Albert Ellis live at the Learning Annex.* New York: 2 cassettes. Institute for Rational-Emotive Therapy.

Ellis, A. (Speaker) (1991). *How to refuse to be angry, vindictive, and unforgiving.* New York: Cassette recording. Institute for Rational-Emotive Therapy.

Epstein, S. (1993). *You're smarter than you think.* New York: Simon & Schuster.

FitzMaurice, K.E. (1989). *Self-concept: The enemy within.* Omaha, NE: FitzMaurice Publishing.

Hauck, P.A. (1973). *Overcoming depression.* Philadelphia: Westminster.

Hauck, P.A. (1974). *Overcoming frustration and anger.* Philadelphia: Westminster.

Hauck, P.A. (1992). *Overcoming the rating game: Beyond self-love— beyond self-esteem.* Louisville, KY: Westminster/John Knox.

Knaus, W. (Speaker) (1975). *Overcoming procrastination.* New York: Cassette recording. Institute for Rational-Emotive Therapy.

Jakubowski, P., & Lange, A. (1978). *The Assertive Option.* Champaign, IL: Research Press.

Korzybski, A. (1933). *Science and sanity.* San Francisco: International Society of General Semantics.

Lange, A., & Jakubowski, P. (1976). *Responsible Assertive Behavior.* Champaign, IL: Research Press.

Lazarus, A., Lazarus, C., & Fay, A. (1993). *Don't believe it for a minute.* San Luis Obispo, CA: Impact.

London, T. (1991). Managing anger. Evanston, IL: Garfield.

Miller, T. (1986). The unfair advantage. Manlius, NY: Horsesense, Inc.

Mills, D. (1993). Overcoming self-esteem. New York: Institute for Rational-Emotive Therapy.

Nottingham, E. (1992). *It's not as bad as it seems.* Memphis: Castle Books.

Sichel, J., & Ellis, A. (1984). *RET self-help form.* New York: Institute for Rational-Emotive Therapy.

Simon, J. (1993). *Good mood.* La Salle, IL: Open Court.

Tate, P. (1993). *Alcohol: How to give it up and be glad you did.* Altamonte Springs, FL: Rational Self-Help Press.

Trimpey, J. (1989). *Rational recovery from alcoholism: The small book.* New York: Bantam.

Trimpey, J., & Trimpey, L. (1990). *Rational recovery from fatness.* Lotus, CA: Lotus Press.

Velten, E. (Speaker) (1989). *How to be unhappy at work.* New York: Cassette recording. Institute for Rational-Emotive Therapy.

Wolfe, J. L. (1993). *What to do when he has a headache.* New York: Penguin.

Wolfe, J. L. (Speaker) (1980). *Woman—Assert yourself.* New York: Cassette recording. Institute for Rational-Emotive Therapy.

Young, H. S. (1974). *A rational counseling primer.* New York: Institute for Rational-Emotive Therapy.

Index

About the Authors

Albert Ellis was born in Pittsburgh and raised in New York City, and holds a bachelor's degree from the City College of New York, and M.A. and Ph.D. degrees in clinical psychology from Columbia University. He has been Adjunct Professor of Psychology at Rutgers University, Pittsburg State University, and other centers of learning, and has served as Chief Psychologist of the New Jersey State Diagnostic Center, and Chief Psychologist of the New Jersey Department of Institutions and Agencies. The founder of rational emotive behavior therapy, he is also the grandfather of cognitive behavior therapy. As of this writing, he is President of the Institute for Rational-Emotive Therapy (New York City), he has practiced psychotherapy, marriage and family therapy, and sex therapy for over 50 years, and continues this multifaceted practice at the Psychological Clinic of the Institute in New York.

Dr. Ellis has published over 600 articles in psychological, psychiatric, and sociological journals and anthologies. He also has authored or edited more than 50 books, including *How to Live With a Neurotic, Reason and Emotion in Psychotherapy, A New Guide to Rational Living, The Practice of Rational-Emotive Therapy,* and *How to Stubbornly Refuse to Make Yourself Miserable About Anything— Yes, Anything!* He presents numerous lectures and workshops in the United States and throughout the rest of the world.

Arthur Lange received his doctorate from American University and completed a postdoctoral internship at Southern Illinois University. He is a Diplomate of the American Board of Professional Psychology. Married and the father of three, he lives with his family on Balboa Island in Newport Beach, California.

As president of Arthur Lange, Inc., Dr. Lange has given over 5,000 presentations using the concepts in this book as applied to self-motivation, exceptional leadership and management, risk-taking, creativity, team-building, personal effectiveness, and managing change. A licensed psychologist, he is the author of two other books (*Responsible Assertive Behavior* and *The Assertive Option*), as well as of numerous articles and chapters. He has made 12 professional films and videos. He is the former director of Psychological Services, and recipient of the Outstanding Teacher Award at the University of California–Irvine.

Dr. Lange presents in the executive management programs at UCLA and the University of California–Riverside. He is in great demand as a substantive (as well as inspiring and entertaining) speaker, both nationally and internationally. His clients include AT&T, NBC, Arco, Nexxus, Nordstrom, Toyota, Hughes, Los Alamos National Lab., Texas Instruments, Baskin–Robbins, Cedars–Sinai Hospital, and The United Way.

More Psychology Books by Dr. Albert Ellis
From Carol Publishing Group